BARONS *of* BUSINESS

BARONS *of* BUSINESS

Their Lives and Lifestyles

For Karen
To celebrate 12-D
January - 2003

William G. Scheller

HUGH LAUTER LEVIN ASSOCIATES, INC.

(PAGE 1)

The Lower Loggia at The Breakers, Newport, Rhode Island.

PHOTO: RICHARD CHEEK FOR THE PRESERVATION SOCIETY OF NEWPORT COUNTY.

(PAGE 2)

The Breakers main gate mid-winter

PHOTO: THE PRESERVATION SOCIETY OF NEWPORT COUNTY.

(PAGE 5)

A garden view of Rockefeller's Kykuit.

USED WITH PERMISSION OF NATIONAL TRUST FOR ISTORIC PRESERVATION. PHOTO © EZRA STOLLER, ESTO PHOTOGRAPHICS.

(PAGE 6)

Malcolm Forbes with one of his Harley Davidsons.

PHOTO COURTESY THE FORBES ARCHIVES. © 2002 ALL RIGHTS RESERVED. PHOTO BY GLEN A. DAVIS.

Copyright © 2002
Hugh Lauter Levin Associates, Inc.
http://www.HLLA.com

Editor: Leslie Conron Carola
Copy Editor: Deborah Teipel Zindell
Designer: Kevin Osborn, Research & Design, Ltd.,
                Arlington, Virginia

Printed in Hong Kong

ISBN: 0-88363-842-8

Contents

Introduction

LONG before the principles of egalitarianism were enshrined in the Declaration of Independence and the Constitution, the settlers of British North America had set a course of social and political development in which hereditary aristocracy would play no significant role. There would be royal charters and land grants, to the likes of the Duke of York and Lord Baltimore; and land itself became something of a patent of nobility in places where it was practical to plant thousands of acres in tobacco or cotton. But the grandees of Spanish America, and the *seigneurs* of New France, would never provide a model for Virginia or New England.

But it wasn't very long before America had an aristocracy, the aristocracy it wanted, the aristocracy its religion (at least in New England) and its system of commerce told it it must have. It wasn't possible for a Puritan to ever know for sure if he or she were one of the elect, predestined for salvation, but worldly success—as long as it wasn't accompanied by prideful extravagance—might be a very good sign that God was smiling upon a person in a spiritual as well as material sense. And the rise of American trade soon made the existence of a wealthy mercantile class inevitable.

As the nineteenth century progressed, the money earned was invested in manufacturing, and then in railroads. Revolutions in printing technology and mass literacy enabled publishing empires to flourish, while urbanization and mass production of consumer goods made retailing a pathway to great riches. New developments in lighting and transportation made oil standard. In the twentieth century, motion pictures and broadcasting, followed by high technology and its information-age applications, created more immense fortunes.

America had its aristocracy, sustained not by looking after bloodlines but by looking out for the main chance. It wasn't hereditary—well, usually for no more than a few generations—but it was as much a part of the national furniture as the House of Lords in Great Britain.

(ABOVE)
The gazebo in the gardens at Lyndhurst.

PHOTO LYNDHURST ARCHIVES, A NATIONAL TRUST HISTORIC SITE.
© LYNDHURST 1999-2002..

(OPPOSITE)
A festive dining table at Skibo Castle, Scotland, home of Andrew Carnegie.

PHOTO SKIBO CASTLE, SCOTLAND.

Britain's Lords have kept their titles, but lost their power. The New World aristocracy had no titles to lose, but its power has never been in doubt. That includes its power to fascinate the rest of us, a power made more tantalizing by the thought of all the main chances that are still out there.

❋ ❋ ❋ ❋ ❋ ❋ ❋ ❋ ❋ ❋ ❋ ❋ ❋ ❋ ❋ ❋ ❋

If there has been a sea change in the ways in which great fortunes are made, it has been more than matched by the style in which they have been spent. This isn't just a matter of the things that money can buy—the difference, say, between a private railroad car and a private jet. It's a matter of how inconspicuously so many of the very rich now consume. This is especially true of individuals who owe their fortunes to business success, as opposed, say, to entertainment or sports celebrity. (That much-ridiculed but nonetheless quite successful 1980s television program "Lifestyles of the Rich and Famous" didn't usually focus on CEOs.) If we look back on '80s binge chronicled in Tom Wolfe's *The Bonfire of the Vanities,* what we recall of most media reportage had to do not with the indulgences of individual magnificoes but with the sudden extravagances of a middle class gotten rich on the cheap: we weren't reading about plutocrats' racehorses, but about the BMW next door.

It has almost gotten to the point where we would like to hear about a tycoon who had furnished his Gulfstream like a private railroad car, in rosewood and velvet—although, puritans that they are, Wall Street's analysts would probably devalue his stock on the grounds that such anachronistic and recherché frivolity probably meant there was a loose nut on the corporate tiller. It's hard to say, though. Some moguls are granted a lot of latitude when it comes to tossing around pots of gold in a less than sobersided fashion. For some reason, balloons often figure into this scheme of indulgence: think of Richard Branson, master of the Virgin empire, who is always trying to set some lighter-than-air flight record; or the late Malcolm Forbes, a balloonist who wasn't interested in records unless it was the record for how much fun a man could have. Nevertheless, both these high fliers always made sure to flaunt the names of their business enterprises on the sides of their big billowing toys. Not only did this put them above the ranks of mere millionaire sportsmen, who have to plaster their balloons with the names of somebody else's watches or champagne; it showed that they could mix business with pleasure.

Why have things changed so completely, over such a relatively short span of years? For one thing, rich people —at least, people who get rich from exercising a genius for business—are better educated, more sophisticated, and simply have better taste. There are no modern counterparts of "Bet-a-Million" Gates, the Gilded-Age sport who brought forty changes of clothes to a Saratoga resort and wore them all in one day.

That's one reason. Another is, quite logically, a desire for privacy, which is inseparable from security. But perhaps the biggest reason of all has to do with the democratization of taste. At one time the only things money could buy, apart from land, were exaggerated versions of the things that most people had—essentially,

clothing, shelter, and transportation. If you were rich, you built a bigger house, filled it with expensive furniture and art, and hired a platoon of servants. You wore elaborate outfits—colorful outfits even if you were a man, at least until 19th-century style-setters decided that black was most becoming. You bought the best horses, and the most ostentatious carriage, that you could afford. And when you were done spending your money, there was no way on earth you could be mistaken for one of the people who worked for you.

This state of affairs persisted until some time in the latter half of the 20th century. Then the old arrangements seemed somehow to be stood on end: instead of factory workers buying suits so they could at least dress like an off-the-rack version of the boss on weekends, we began to see Sam Walton in a pickup truck, Steven Spielberg in a ball cap and sneakers, and Ted Turner pulling a plug of chewing tobacco out of his jeans. More than top hats have gone out of style—the top hat mentality has vanished as well.

With the exception of a few ascetics, the rich still have their houses and cars—but they are no longer on display. A freestanding mansion on Fifth Avenue would be unthinkable today, even if it weren't out of reach of all but a half-dozen super-moguls. Too many people would stare in the windows, or worse. Now we do our looking from a somewhat greater distance, and we treasure our few wealthy exhibitionists more than ever. They give us the enjoyment we once had watching Cornelius Vanderbilt careen along behind a pair of fast trotters, or squinting seaward as *Cleopatra's Barge* , the Crowninshield yacht, wafted into Salem harbor.

The Yankee Ships Were Everywhere

NORTH American civilization came into existence at a turning point in the history of moneymaking. For centuries, land ownership had been the foundation of wealth, with trade—financed by the system of investment banking pioneered in late medieval Italy—only beginning to create a class of magnificoes to rival the landholding, and usually titled, classes. Industrial capitalism loomed on the horizon, but it was a horizon yet to be blurred by coal smoke and steam.

The European colonies in North America clustered tightly along the seacoasts, and along great rivers such as the Hudson and the St. Lawrence. Where the land was fertile, and where it was easy for crops to be siphoned toward the sea lanes, colonists ventured farther from the ocean. The great plantations of tidewater Maryland and Virginia, the Dutch patroonships of the Hudson valley, and the French seigneuries along the St. Lawrence all helped to create the first great North American fortunes, although in many cases these vast landholdings were granted to men who were already secure members of the European aristocracies. In the American South, plantation agriculture created its own small aristocracy—but one which, fertile as it was in yielding brainpower and military genius for the Revolution, provided no business model for the busy centuries to come. The true barons of American business first appeared in that corner of the continent where breaking out into broad agricultural hinterlands was most difficult, and where money had to be made in commerce if it was to be made at all.

To this day, the coast of New England is graced with the handsome 18th-century homes of shipowners and sea captains who took risks upon the North Atlantic and beyond, and who turned their profits into fine architecture, exquisite furniture, and old Madeira. Walk the streets of Portsmouth, New Hampshire, or Newburyport, Massachusetts—to name just two of the towns that bred the race of

Yankee traders—and the style of the era and the
opportunities it afforded are impossible to ignore.

THE HANCOCKS

In the largest of those seaports of colonial New
England, on the slopes of the highest hill, stood one of
the grandest of all those princely merchants' homes.
It isn't there any longer—the 19th century didn't share
today's passion for historic preservation—but the
surname of the man who built it looms large, in both the
literal and figurative sense, in the history of the United
States. Thomas Hancock was the son of a respected
pastor in Cambridge, Massachusetts, across the Charles
River from Boston. The path that led to his Beacon
Hill mansion began with the decision that he would not
follow his father into the ministry, as his brother John
would, but instead would cross the river to Boston and
apprentice to a bookseller. This was in 1717, when
Thomas was 14 years of age. John was already at
Harvard, and tuition for two was possibly too much
of a drain on a pastor's salary. Reverend Hancock might
also have seen that his second son's talents had a
worldly rather than a spiritual bent.

Thomas Hancock served his bookseller master for
seven years, learning everything from printing to
binding to retail sales. At the end of his apprenticeship
he opened his own shop, but the book business was too
narrow to contain him. By 1727, he was dabbling in
the long-distance transport and sale of general
merchandise; the next year, he and several partners
built a paper mill just south of Boston. In 1731,
Hancock married Lydia Henchman, the daughter of

The drawing room in Boston's 1796 Harrison Gray Otis House, first of Otis's three Bulfinch-designed homes.

PHOTO COURTESY THE SOCIETY FOR THE PRESERVATION OF NEW ENGLAND ANTIQUITIES, BOSTON.

one of his paper mill associates. To his native ambition—which by now included his first dabblings in politics—Thomas Hancock now added a matrimonial connection to a well-to-do family.

Bookselling became less and less of a factor in the Hancock enterprises, as the entrepreneur moved into land speculation and importing. In the Boston of the mid-1730s—a town barely a century old, but already a far cry from the cramped little theocracy of its early days—the name Hancock was one that was recognized on the docks and in the counting houses. Thomas Hancock needed a residence to match his station, and in 1736 he began building it on Beacon Hill.

For the past two centuries, a Beacon Hill address has been the *ne plus ultra* of social standing in Boston. But the brick row houses built along Beacon Street ("the sunny street that holds the sifted few," as the first Oliver Wendell Holmes called it) and adjacent streets came along later than Thomas Hancock's day; these were part of the development that followed the removal of the hill's steep summit and the building of Charles Bulfinch's magnificent Massachusetts State House in the late 1790s. The Beacon Hill on which Thomas Hancock bought property and built his mansion was very much the Boston outskirts in the 1730s; off on his own, surrounded by orchards and gardens that trailed down the hill's south slope to Boston Common, Hancock could enjoy town and harbor views yet at the same time feel as if he were living out in the countryside.

The house was Georgian, with the cool symmetry and gambrel roof characteristic of the style, and it was

An Otis House interior: careful documentation
has revealed the Federal era's love of vivid colors.

sumptuously large for its era. Its two and a half stories contained a dozen or more principal rooms, with smaller chambers serving as quarters for servants and slaves (slavery was still legal in the Massachusetts of that era) and for such necessities as the storage of china. Fine porcelain, along with silver (the French Huguenot émigré Apollos Revere and his son, Paul, did lovely custom work in 18th-century Boston) and polished mahogany were prime tokens of success among the merchant princes of the day.

And so were fine carriages. Here Thomas Hancock really went over the top, ordering a coach that took its London manufacturer three years to build and ship. Hancock went into great detail about everything from size (it had to be big enough to accommodate his wife, a tall, heavy woman) to upholstery (scarlet or a light color, "whichever is most fashionable") to windows designed to incorporate sliding panels of both glass and canvas. Even the harnesses and bells were custom made, as befit Hancock's station.

Thomas Hancock died in 1764. His principal heir was his nephew, the son of Thomas's late brother. Like his father and grandfather, the young man's name was John. Educated at Harvard and polished with a tour of England at his uncle's expense, taught the intricacies of commerce and the ways of a gentleman, John Hancock became at age 27 heir to a fortune estimated at half a million dollars. Over the next 30 years, he would rule Boston society from the house on Beacon Hill, eventually serving as governor of Massachusetts. Along the way, he would become that rare thing among the rich and privileged—at least those who do not renounce their fortunes, as John Hancock

assuredly did not. He would become famous as a political revolutionary, a man whose grand signature would scream defiance at the British crown.

But John Hancock's career as a revolutionary and patriot was still 10 years in the future at the time he came into his inheritance. Throughout the 1760s and early 1770s, Hancock was busy with his role as a Boston selectman—and, later, a member of the Massachusetts legislature—and with keeping his business solvent in the face of an economic downturn made worse by the Sugar and Stamp acts imposed by the British upon the colonies. As with most of the future revolutionaries, independence was the furthest thing from Hancock's mind as he threaded his way through the tangle of growing injustices, most connected with taxes and restrictions on trade, that ultimately led to the outbreak of rebellion. By the time the die was cast, and Hancock was ready to affix that famous signature to the Declaration of Independence, he perhaps more than any of the other Founders gave the American Revolution its character as essentially a bourgeois, rather than a radical insurrection.

John Hancock might be a political bedfellow of the populist Sam Adams, but his aristocratic style didn't suffer at all. In fact—and the 1960s term "limousine liberal" might occur to us at this juncture—he seamlessly merged his image as a magnifico with that of the friend of the common man. He wheeled through the streets of Boston in Uncle Thomas's coach, impeccably attired in the best wigs and waistcoats, jeweled or even solid gold buttons gleaming; to keep his frequent entertainments lubricated, he might order 400 gallons of the best Madeira at a time to stock the Beacon Street cellars.

was over—years that included his terms as governor of Massachusetts—his profligate spending continued until he had worked his way nearly to the bottom of his inheritance and whatever money he had made on his own. When he died in 1793, Boston society was astounded to learn that "King Hancock" had not even left a will. What remained of his fortune was largely in land, including the Beacon Hill mansion. It was a sad postscript to John Hancock's short, showy life that the mansion his Uncle Thomas had built was demolished in 1863, when the property was taken for back taxes. If it had been spared, it would stand today just to the left of the State House, where, with its memories of flowing Madeira and the clatter of that regal carriage, it might have provided a vivid contrast with later gubernatorial preferences. Michael Dukakis, remember, used to ride the subways.

So it was with John Hancock, and with the other merchant princes of early New England. Their ostentation mostly came down to homes and furniture, food and drink, and fine apparel. As for that last item, remember that the 18th century was not the era of casual Fridays; nor were dress clothes limited to a palette of grays and blues. Take a look at Nicholas Boylston, Boston's premier importer of luxury goods, as painted in 1767 by John Singleton Copley. Lounging in his study, his arm resting on a ledger and a painting of a merchant ship behind him, his expression an odd mixture of impatience and nonchalance, the mogul wears a blue waistcoat, a brown damask dressing gown, and a red velvet turban to keep the chill off his shaven head (it's early morning, no doubt, and his valet hasn't

And yet he could stand before a gathering and denounce "the glare of wealth" and extol the virtues of poverty. Few seemed to mind, because John Hancock was a generous man. His ample bequests to Harvard College included a thousand books; he gave the city of Boston a fire engine, provided furnishings for churches, and donated firewood to the poor.

John Hancock's fortune survived the Revolution, but in the 10 years of life he had left after the conflict

yet helped him with his wig). Such displays of male sartorial gorgeousness were *de riguer* among Boylston's set. John Hancock, as we saw, always made sure to cut a fine figure; and Harrison Gray Otis, a nabob of the next generation, wore gold lace in his hats.

HARRISON GRAY OTIS

Otis's is a name to be reckoned with when it comes to that other hallmark of high early American society, fine architecture. He had three houses built for himself, on and around Beacon Hill, within eight years beginning in 1796. Each was designed by the incomparable Charles Bulfinch in the chastely elegant Federal style, that miracle of proportioning and exquisite yet restrained detailing whereby an ostensible square box becomes a thing of lightness and loveliness. The first Otis house is on Cambridge Street, and is now the headquarters of the Society for the Preservation of New England Antiquities; its interior is resplendent in the bright, striking colors of the Federal era. The second—the only free-standing mansion surviving on Beacon Hill— is still a private home on Mt. Vernon Street. The last of the three, where the land speculator and congressman lived from 1804 until his death in 1848, stands on Beacon Street. It is the headquarters of the American Meteorological Society. Unlike Harrison Gray Otis, the meteorologists do not keep a perpetually filled Lowestoft porcelain punch bowl at the foot of the stairs. That might make the weather altogether too agreeable, all of the time.

Speaking of Otis, and of food and drink, we should note that he ate not three but four meals a day—and the first was generally a breakfast that included paté de foie gras.

❊ ❊ ❊ ❊ ❊ ❊ ❊ ❊ ❊ ❊ ❊ ❊ ❊ ❊ ❊ ❊ ❊ ❊

Boston may have remained the political capital of Massachusetts, but in the decades immediately following the winning of American independence, the port of Salem, some 15 miles north of Boston, became the mercantile center of the American universe. Poor Salem—it's ironic that when we think of it today, we tend to concentrate on the least savory part of its history, the 1690s witch trials that centered upon what is today part of the nearby town of Danvers. This is partly Salem's own fault, as it plays up its witch connections for the sake of tourism in what must be the world's only example of a successful attempt to lure visitors by recalling an instance of cruel persecution. But Salem's real fame ought to rest on its one-time status as a fabulously wealthy port—a mercantile hive so successful that there were Chinese traders, accustomed to dealing with their Yankee counterparts from Salem, who thought that the city must be a great

nation all its own. Indeed, on one Chinese map drawn 200 years ago, the word "Salem" sprawls across the entire eastern portion of the United States.

These were the days when "the Yankee ships were everywhere." So wrote Esther Forbes in her biography, *Paul Revere and the World He Lived In.* Forbes was referring to the fact that by the time of Revere's death, in 1818, bells made at his foundry in Canton, Massachusetts, might be heard not only in New England steeples, but on board ships "under the strange shadow of Java Head or in the cruel Straits of Sunda." The very ubiquity of Revere's bells suggests that the old patriot had struck upon a far more lucrative career than custom silversmithing, and had fallen into step with the way great fortunes would be made during the century just beginning. But between the end of the American Revolution and the 1820s—with a hiatus during the unpopular embargo leading up to the War of 1812 and the war itself—shipping was the path to American riches, and Salem was the place where that path most promisingly began.

ELIAS HASKET DERBY

Salem's wharves begat Thomas Handasyd Perkins, who turned down George Washington's offer to make him secretary of the Navy on the grounds that he was already in command of a larger fleet of ships. And Salem was the first American city to produce a millionaire. That was one Elias Hasket Derby, known in his day as "King" Derby. (Americans in those days were glad to get rid of a real king, but they clung to the sobriquet when it came to their Hancocks and Derbys.)

Like Hancock, Derby stood on another man's shoulders when it came to acquiring his fortune—in this case his father, Richard Derby, a prosperous pre-Revolutionary merchant whose 1762 home, the oldest brick house in Salem, survives on the grounds of the Salem Maritime National Historic Site (the site also includes Derby Wharf, and the 1819 Custom House made famous by Nathaniel Hawthorne in *The Scarlet Letter*). With its trim dormers, finely dentiled cornice, and 12-over-12 windows, the Derby House is classic Georgian, very much along the lines of the lost Hancock mansion in Boston if not as large. From those windows, Richard Derby could enjoy the finest harbor views imaginable: his own ships, coming and going, and unloading their lucrative cargoes at his namesake wharf.

With the coming of the Revolution, more than a few of those ships were privateers. Elias Hasket Derby was by this time fully engaged in his father's business, and he himself became one of America's most effective carriers of letters of marque. Once the war was over, he lost not a moment in converting to peacetime commerce. In 1785 he sent his one-time privateer *Grand Turk* into the East India trade, launching a series of voyages so profitable it was said the younger Derby was regularly accustomed to a 100 percent return.

Lord help anyone, in fact, who worked for King Derby and failed to step lively enough to facilitate such enormous profits. Derby was not the sort of man you would want to present with a sloppy expense account—or, for that matter, with any expense account at all. He regularly required his ships' captains to engage in enough side business to cover all expenses, so that his profits would be pure and unencumbered.

Elias Hasket Derby was a tall, dour man with formal, old-fashioned manners and a presence that combined stateliness with swagger. He carried a gold-headed cane and wore buckles studded with diamonds. He built what might have been the finest house in Salem—judging from the Federal-era architectural treasures that city still possesses, that would have been quite the superlative—but he built it primarily to please his wife, Elizabeth Crowninshield. One of the quirks of this particular Derby mansion was its black marble staircase, seven feet wide. It seems that Elizabeth Crowninshield Derby was chilled by the thought of her coffin someday being carried down the stairs at an unseemly angle, either head or feet first. So she specified a staircase wide enough to accommodate her remains at level broadside.

Elias Hasket Derby's real love (apart from his ships and Elizabeth, likely in that order) was his farm in suburban Danvers, where his greenhouses were planted in strawberries and lemons. Here he kept a curious artifact. It was a wooden effigy of a hermit, seated in a bark hut with a hermit's scant portion of bread and water before it. In the statue's hands was an open book inscribed, "Give me neither poverty or riches." Elias Hasket Derby, of course, had swerved radically toward one of those options rather than the other. His descendants swerved just as radically in the other direction: King Derby died in 1799, his million-dollar-plus fortune intact (Elizabeth had already taken her last dignified trip downstairs); but his sons were profligates who quickly ran through their inheritance. In 1810, the Derby mansion in Salem was demolished, for want of anyone who cared or could afford to keep it up.

THE CROWNINSHIELDS

The Crowninshields, the family that had produced Elizabeth Crowninshield Derby of the seven-foot-wide black marble staircase, were another Salem merchant family of legend. The first Crowninshield of any consequence was named John, who usually spelled his name "Grouncell" in the odd orthography of the 18th century. He was the son of a mysterious Doctor Johann von Kronenscheldt, who had turned up in Boston in 1684—he claimed to be a German nobleman, but no one has ever known for sure just who he was, where he came from, or whether he was an actual doctor even by the standards of the day—and settled in the town of Lynn, located midway between Boston and Salem.

John Grouncell was no merchant prince. He was primarily a fisherman and a smuggler, and he is remembered in Salem today as the builder of the 1727 Crowninshield-Bentley House, a modest early jewel in a Peabody-Essex Museum collection crowned by the great Federal mansions designed by Samuel McIntire for later shipping magnates. Grouncell/Crowninshield's son, George, started out modestly enough. He worked as a captain on ships belonging to King Derby, whose sister he had married. (His own sister was Elizabeth, Derby's wife.)

But by the 1790s, George Crowninshield was a shipowner himself. His favored cargo was pepper, which he and his captains bought along the west coast

of Sumatra in what is now Indonesia. The pepper trade was a tricky business, requiring the Yankee captains to employ all their wits against wily Malay suppliers, British competitors, and each other. But George Crowninshield was up to the challenge. In 1801, two of his ships brought more than a million pounds of pepper into Salem harbor. During the decade that followed, he and his sons came to think of Sumatra as "our pepper gardens." A lucrative coffee trade with India followed, and by 1810 the family had supplanted the Derbys as the lords of Salem's commerce.

George's sons were all agents of the family firm. One, Jacob, became a U.S. congressman to whom Thomas Jefferson in 1804 offered the post of secretary of the Navy. He declined—the second Salem shipping tycoon to place his private seafaring concerns above responsibility for those of the nation. (His brother, Benjamin, took the job under James Madison in 1814.) The Crowninshields, as it turned out, had a navy of their own: during the War of 1812, six of the family's privateer vessels captured or sank more than 80 British ships.

Ultimately, it was neither a merchant ship nor a naval vessel that gave those early Crowninshields a unique place in the history of American seafaring. It was a yacht—the first ship in the nation built purely for pleasure.

George Crowninshield, Jr., was George Crowninshield's eldest son. A lifelong bachelor, he stayed home and helped run the Salem end of the family's far-flung operations, specializing in outfitting ships. With the development of his inner life hampered by the fact that he was nearly illiterate, he indulged a love of outward display. He drove a bright yellow carriage around Salem; he wore high tasseled boots, splashy waistcoats, and a powdered pigtail.

The career of the younger George Crowninshield offers one of America's first examples of wealth and industry ripening into eccentricity and decadence. By the time George, Sr., died in 1815, the family fortune was secure and, with three surviving brothers to help run things, there really wasn't much for the younger George to do. His legacy thus became not that of a firm hand on the levers of business, but on the tiller of his one spectacular indulgence—the yacht called *Cleopatra's Barge*.

Along with ceremony and display, George Crowninshield, Jr., loved the glamour of celebrity—especially titled celebrity. He had a particular fascination with Napoleon, and with Charlotte, Princess of Wales. Accordingly he hatched the idea of building a pleasure yacht and sailing it to Europe, hoping to attract visits from as many royal or at least noble

A replica of the main cabin of Cleopatra's Barge, *as displayed in Salem's Peabody-Essex Museum.*

personages as possible. Perhaps, if the princess or someone equally glamorous were sufficiently impressed, he or she might be persuaded to accompany the yachtsman back to Salem. (Napoleon was unavailable, having already been exiled to St. Helena.)

Cleopatra's Barge was launched at Salem in October of 1816. She was a hermaphroditic brigantine (the name applies to a ship square-rigged on the foremast and rigged with a triangular fore-and-aft sail on the mainmast). She was the size of a small warship—83 feet long at the waterline, nearly 23 feet across at the beam, and weighing almost 200 tons. Her hull was a riot of color: one side was painted in horizontal bands, the other in a herringbone pattern, and there was gold leaf everywhere. The cabins and salons of the *Barge* would have done credit to a McIntire mansion: no expense was spared on carpets, on settees upholstered in velvet, on gilt mirrors, or on maple and mahogany paneling. The ceiling beams were edged in gilt beading; velvet ropes bound with gold cord were slung along the bulkheads to provide a grip for passengers in rough seas. The best porcelain, crystal, silver, and linen graced the dining salon.

Outfitted with a liveried crew, captained by George's cousin Benjamin Crowninshield, *Cleopatra's Barge* slipped out of Salem harbor on March 30, 1817, carrying her strange owner on a strange, glamour-seeking voyage.

It was a voyage of disappointment. A German baron and a British lord were entertained on board at Genoa, and Crowninshield did get to meet the mother, sister, brother, and uncle of Napoleon. At Elba, the deposed French emperor's erstwhile place of exile, the hero-worshiper from Salem even managed to buy a few of Napoleon's abandoned possessions, including a pair of his boots. But there had been no luck in contacting Marie Louise, Napoleon's estranged empress, nor the princess of Wales. And as a final insult, the supposed "adopted son" of Bonaparte, invited to sail to America on *Cleopatra's Barge*, turned out to be an impostor.

The *Barge* dropped anchor in Salem harbor in early October. George Crowninshield almost immediately began planning another cruise, but it never got under way. A little more than a month after his return, the pixilated scion of the House of Crowninshield dropped dead in the galley of his folly of a yacht.

Cleopatra's Barge did not long survive her master. By 1820 she was the property of Kamehameha, king of Hawaii, and she was lost on a reef (the king was not aboard) four years later. But a tribute to her splendor may be seen in her home port: replicas of the main cabin, and the master stateroom with its canopied bed, are on display at Salem's Peabody-Essex Museum.

THE BROWN BROTHERS

The Rhode Island cities of Providence and Newport were also bastions of trade in the 18th and early 19th centuries. In Providence, the name to conjure with was Brown—a name associated with the city to this day, through the family's role in creating and supporting Brown University.

Four Brown brothers came to maturity in the Providence of the mid- to late-1700s, sons of a merchant who had also dabbled in whaling, distilling, farming,

and slave trading. After the father's death, the four
boys—John, Moses, Joseph, and Nicholas (a fifth,
James, died as a very young man)—worked for an
uncle, Obadiah Brown, whose activities included
shipping and candlemaking. Eventually, Obadiah
and his nephews would become colonial America's
largest manufacturers of candles.

The Brown brothers prospered mightily in the
shipping and candlemaking enterprises, which they
inherited and managed with considerable harmony
following their uncle's death in 1762. But as the years
progressed, their individual personalities asserted
themselves . . . most significantly, around the issue
of slavery.

At first, all of the Brown brothers had benefited from
the slave trade. Just three years after coming
into their inheritance, Moses, Joseph, and John
collaborated in fitting out a brig for a slaving voyage. In
the years that followed, slaving loomed ever larger
as a component of John Brown's income. Around the
same time, Nicholas dabbled in the trade, but later
became a firm opponent. Joseph, as he grew older, took
less and less interest in business, preferring scientific
pursuits and architecture. Moses, meanwhile, came to
have the strongest misgivings of all regarding the
commerce in human lives: he taught his own slaves to
read and write, and gave them their freedom following
his midlife conversion to Quakerism. Thereafter he
became a leader in the anti-slavery movement, a position
that put him in dire opposition to his brother, John.
John Brown wasn't a reticent slaver, content to bank his
profits while keeping quiet about their source; he was an

active opponent of anti-slavery legislation. The wonder
is that the brothers kept talking to each other. Moses
and John remained quite close in the years prior to
John's death in 1803. (Moses outlived all of his brothers,
dying in 1836 at age 97.)

Aside from Brown University, the greatest tangible
reminder of the years of the Brown brothers' ascendancy
in Providence is the house that Joseph Brown designed
for his brother, John, in 1786. John Quincy Adams
called it "the most magnificent and elegant private
mansion that I have ever seen on this continent." Adams
was not given to exaggeration, and his words might well
stand today: even though many a larger home has been
built in North America over the past two centuries, few
if any are more "magnificent and elegant."

The three-story, 12-room Brown house brings the
classical regularity of high Georgian architecture to its
pinnacle in this hemisphere. The central block of the
building projects outwards, enhancing the imposing
doorway and the lovely Palladian window on the
second floor; above, the building's height is accentuated
by a balustrade surrounding the roof. Inside, amid
exquisite paneling and pedimented doorways, is a
superb collection of 18th-century furniture and Chinese
porcelain—a reminder that, in addition to slave trading,
John Brown's fortune was built on his pioneering of the
immensely lucrative China trade.

The proprietor of all this magnificence must have
been a little rough on the furniture. John Brown was an
immense specimen. He was so big that he took up the
entire seat in his chaise; when his grandchildren rode
with him, they had to sit on the floor between his legs.

JOHN JACOB ASTOR

The subway stop at Astor Place, across from Cooper
Union in New York's East Village, is one of those old
stations that still preserves the cool white tile walls of a
century ago. Set amid the tiles in one of those walls is a
curious plaque, which appears to have nothing to do
with either subways or the world upstairs. It depicts a
beaver gnawing on a stick. Its reference is to a tough
little German immigrant, and to one of the greatest
American fortunes.

Drop one "l", and the name of the village where
John Jacob Astor was born in 1763 has a decided New
York ring. Walldorf is in the province of Baden, and it
was there that Astor's father, John Jacob, Sr., ran a
butcher shop that might well have turned out to be the
younger man's livelihood as well. Instead of cattle and
pigs, though, there were beaver pelts in John Jacob
Astor's future—beaver pelts, and an immense amount of
real estate.

Astor came to the United States in 1784 by way of
London, where he had worked for an older brother in
the musical instrument business. He brought a
consignment of flutes across the Atlantic, and sold them
on the side while he worked for a fur dealer. Soon the
two businesses intertwined, as Astor invested profits
from importing and selling instruments in his first fur-
buying trip to upstate New York.

Astor made connections in Montreal, capital of the
North American fur trade, and expanded his business
exporting pelts to the lucrative London market. In the
late 1700s, the three dollars a beaver pelt fetched could

John Jacob Astor's fur-trading enterprise led to the establishment of the first American fur monopoly in the United States.

buy a musket, which could be traded to the Indians for 10 more pelts. With that rate of return working in his favor, Astor entered the China trade around 1800—a year when, after 16 years in America, he was already worth $100,000. Furs went to China; tea and silk came back. The exchange brought the coarse, crafty German immigrant an enormous profit, $300,000 of which he promptly sunk into what was by no means considered a prudent investment in that first decade of the 1800s: Manhattan real estate.

Buying and selling acreage in the yet-to-be-settled parts of New York City was an amusing pastime—later, Astor would hold his property and sublet it for development—but furs were still the main event. The American acquisition of the Louisiana Territory, and its exploration by Lewis and Clark, paved the way for Astor's creation of a string of fur-trading posts on the Columbia River and the creation of the port called Astoria where that river empties into the Pacific.

John Jacob Astor, through his American Fur Company, became America's first monopolist and its first multimillionaire. But he sold his interest in

American Fur in 1834, and from then on it was real estate all the way. Just how much money stood to be made from investing in the land the burgeoning metropolis stood on is apparent from a simple set of figures: in 1832, the assessed value of the city's property was $104 million. In 1836, the figure was $253 million. Astor bought land all over the city; and he was not averse to adding to his holdings through foreclosure. He didn't build on his property, but leased to others who did. The only building he constructed, aside from his own residence, was the Astor House Hotel. (Both the old and the present Waldorf-Astoria hotels, which commemorate both his name and his hometown, were built long after his death.)

Few people ever praised John Jacob Astor for his generosity, or made note of his self-indulgence. Cited by biographer Virginia Cowles as being "so niggardly it was almost pathological," he kept an eye on every dime. His only personal indulgence seems to have been the theater; he became part owner of the Park Theater in 1806, and rebuilt it when it burned in 1820. Presumably, he liked the idea of being able to enjoy a play now and then while saving money on his own tickets and charging others for theirs. His other pastimes didn't extend much beyond an after-dinner pipe and glass of beer, listening to music, an occasional game of checkers, and riding his horse around town. Aside from the fact that those rides often had the ulterior purpose of scouting out real estate, Astor's modest amusements might easily have been those of the middle-class butcher he had originally apprenticed to be.

John Jacob Astor IV, great-grandson of John Jacob and son of William Backhouse Astor, Jr., and Caroline Schermerhorn Astor, the Mrs. Astor who devised the famous "400"—a list of families and individuals whose lineage could be traced back at least three generations.
PHOTO LIBRARY OF CONGRESS.

Things weren't much different when it came to spending money on others. Astor provided well for his family, including a son and namesake who suffered from a lifelong mental condition, and he kept a comfortable household and ample table. But he was tightfisted with business associates and strangers. He once refused to pay $500 for a chronometer—a timekeeping device crucial for establishing longitude—for one of his ships, saying it was the captain's responsibility. The captain quit. An oft-repeated story has it that a petitioner for charity, disappointed with the five dollars Astor gave

him, pointed out that Astor's son, William Backhouse Astor, had given him ten dollars. "He can afford to," the old man replied. "He has a rich father." Astor even felt the need to comment on others' spendthrift habits: he once predicted a new hotel would fail because the management provided lumps of sugar that were too large.

In the end, the squat old tycoon—his once-wiry frame had filled out so that he looked the part of the beefy, aging butcher—did manage a bequest of nearly a half-million dollars to found the Astor Library (since incorporated into the New York Public Library), along with smaller sums for lesser institutions for his hometown of Walldorf. His legacy of between $20 and $30 million dollars left his family so well provided for that Astor remains to this day a synonym for inherited wealth. But when he was near death, at the age of 84 in 1848, he was still insisting that his agents pursue tenants for overdue rents.

THE DU PONTS OF DELAWARE

Another European immigrant, a man of much more substantial means than the young John Jacob Astor, arrived in the United States in 1800. In fact, Eleuthère Irénée du Pont de Nemours was perhaps alone among the aristocrats of American business in actually having *been* an aristocrat: his family belonged to the minor French nobility, and his father, Pierre, had been a distinguished diplomat who was involved in the secret negotiations that led to British acknowledgment of American independence in 1783.

Pierre du Pont brought his family to America to seek refuge from the excesses of the French Revolution, whose leaders of the moment he and his son Eleuthère had offended by publishing politically moderate tracts. The younger du Pont (he was 29 when he emigrated) did know his way around a printing press, but he was primarily a scientist. He listed his occupation as "botanist" on his immigration papers, and he did in fact bring along a number of young chestnut trees (he continued to import chestnuts, hybridized them, and planted them throughout New Jersey and Delaware). But Eleuthère Irénée du Pont was first and foremost a chemist. His particular expertise was with gunpowder, the manufacture of which he had studied with the great French scientist Antoine Lavoisier.

On a cold, damp day in the winter of 1801, E. I. du Pont was hunting in the woodlands around the Pennsylvania–Delaware border. His rifle continually misfired because of the moist air, and his day's sport was ruined. But he didn't blame the weather. He blamed his powder, which absorbed the dampness, and he decided he could use his French training to create a better product.

Using waterpower from Delaware's Brandywine River, E. I. du Pont set up his first black powder mill near Wilmington in 1802 and started selling his product two years later. The venture was well timed: the War of 1812 was just around the corner, and there was a frontier to be pushed back. But E. I. du Pont doesn't seem to have been just another munitions profiteer. For one thing, he was concerned with overall agricultural and silvicultural improvements to his adopted nation—witness all those chestnut trees, and the fact that he introduced Spanish merino sheep to the U.S. to improve the wool supply. He was also interested in the welfare of his workers, and underlined his emphasis on safety by building his own family's home right on the Brandywine, near the powder mills. The family of any employee killed in an explosion was given free tenure in a company-owned house for the rest of their lives, with guaranteed employment for the victim's children.

Ironically, one of E. I. du Pont's own sons was killed in a mishap involving his famously volatile product. And, as if reflecting that early company policy, members of the du Pont family have found two centuries of employment with the mammoth chemical company founded by the "botanist" who fled the French Revolution.

✽ ✽ ✽ ✽ ✽ ✽ ✽ ✽ ✽ ✽ ✽ ✽ ✽ ✽ ✽

Back in New England, all of that money from the China and East India trades had to go somewhere. The sharpest minds among the old merchant aristocracy soon came to understand that the 19th century's new technologies would favor not merely those who bought and sold, but those who made things. Two of those burgeoning technologies were the mass production of textiles, and the railroad. Yankee money found its way into both.

One Dr. John Collins Bossidy—the name suggests that other dominant ethnic strain in Boston's history— once tweaked the city's Brahmin establishment with a toast:

(OPPOSITE)

The grand staircase at Nemours, the 102-room Wilmington, Delaware, chateau built by Alfred L. du Pont in 1910.

(PREVIOUS SPREAD)

The Chinese parlor at Winterthur was a favorite place for du Pont gatherings. The original 1837 home was substantially enlarged.

(ABOVE)

The library at Nemours, with its finely carved paneling and warm colors, welcomed company and encouraged reflection.

And this is good old Boston,

    The home of the bean and the cod,

  Where the Lowells talk only to the Cabots

    And the Cabots talk only to God.

Francis Cabot Lowell could talk in both directions. This possessor of two of the most formidable names in Yankeedom, and of a good portion of the mercantile fortunes their bearers had amassed, lived at the beginning of the textile revolution.

An Englishman named Samuel Slater had brought the rudiments of mechanized spinning technology to the United States in 1793—you can still visit his mill, on the banks of the Blackstone River in Pawtucket, Rhode Island—and no less a personage than Moses Brown went into business with him. But the American textile industry got its greatest boost when Francis Cabot Lowell came home from a trip to England in 1812 with the working details of that nation's greatest economic treasure tucked into his copious mind. This was the power loom, a device so vital to English industry that its export—or even the export of plans for its construction—was strictly forbidden. Working from memory, Lowell built and patented his own loom. It went into service at Waltham, Massachusetts, in 1814, and, on a larger scale, in the mills established at the entrepreneur's namesake city of Lowell beginning in the 1820s. (Lowell had died, still a relatively young man, in 1817.)

Francis Cabot Lowell must have been a gregarious, clubbable sort during his salad days. He was one of the founders of the most elite of Harvard's undergraduate clubs, the Porcellian, which was originally named the Pig Club because Lowell and fellow founder Robert Treat Paine liked roast pork. As he matured, he seems to have become something of a workaholic. Expecting no less of a commitment from his mill operatives, he nevertheless helped pioneer the idea of factory towns as model communities, in which religious, educational, and social advantages would prevent the vice and misery associated with the English manufacturing cities.

His partner, Nathan Appleton, another Boston Yankee with family shipping money behind him, continued to promote such ideas during the development of the city of Lowell with its model boardinghouses for young, mostly female "operatives." (This was before rapidly expanding business made immigrant labor—and struggles over such niceties as the 13-hour day—inevitable.) Appleton, a scholar and amateur economist, a book collector and keeper of a conversational salon, was also a Brahmin of iron will and purpose. The day before he died, in 1861, he attended the funeral of his daughter. Fanny Appleton Longfellow, wife of the poet, had burned to death in a home accident involving a candle. The same day, Appleton's doctor told him he had two days to live. The old Yankee died on Sunday, only a little ahead of schedule, having told a friend not to bother coming to see him on Monday. "I am not," he had said that weekend, "afraid of anything." He needn't have worried about his elegant, Bulfinch-designed Federal mansion at 39 Beacon Street. The brick bowfronted building has

been kept in fine repair by the Women's City Club of Boston, and is occasionally open for tours.

John Murray Forbes was another heir to an impeccable Boston Brahmin name, and a man distinguished by having personally bridged the China trade and railroad eras. Back when the 19th century was young, Forbes had sailed in Massachusetts vessels bound for Canton and made his fortune before he was 24. As he and the century matured, he took his money and put it on the rails. He led a group of venture capitalists that bought the financially tottering Michigan Central and drove it through to Chicago; with this entry point to the Midwest secured, he bought a short line railroad and expanded it until it became the Chicago, Burlington, and Quincy. Forbes appears to have packed up his Puritan sense of rectitude and probity and brought it west with him. His friend Ralph Waldo Emerson once remarked, apropos of Forbes's integrity, that he was "not likely, in any company, to meet a man superior to himself." Boston could rise to the occasion of the railroads, but it had trouble coming by the robber baron image.

(ABOVE)

Longwood Gardens, created by Pierre S. du Pont, has more fountains than any other American garden.

PHOTO LARRY ALBEE/LONGWOOD GARDENS, PENNSYLVANIA.

(RIGHT)

The 1,050-acre Longwood complex boasts 11,000 plant varieties in 20 outdoor and 20 indoor gardens.

PHOTO LARRY ALBEE/LONGWOOD GARDENS, PENNSYLVANIA.

The Gilded Age

GROWING UP on the family farm on Staten Island, Cornelius Vanderbilt learned how to handle boats while taking produce across to Manhattan for his father. In 1810 the 16-year-old boy pestered his parents for the loan of $100 to buy a small sailboat of the type called a periauger. Buying his own small craft, "Cornele" figured, would be a ticket off the farm and into a lucrative business ferrying passengers and goods across the Narrows. It was a ticket, indeed . . . a ticket to a fleet of ships that would earn him the nickname "Commodore," to mastery of a system of transportation yet to be invented, and to the greatest fortune amassed by any American of his day.

"I didn't feel as much real satisfaction when I made two million in that Harlem [Railroad] corner," said Cornelius Vanderbilt late in life, "as I did on that bright May morning sixty years before when I stepped into my own periauger, hoisted my own sail, and put my hand on my own tiller."

"Commodore" Cornelius Vanderbilt's hand was always on the tiller. Most of his life, and the bulk of his career, took place before the giddy decades of success and excess that Mark Twain and Charles Dudley Warner dubbed the "Gilded Age." But in many ways, the Commodore set the tone for that era, and he was the first overarching figure in the industry that drove the age.

"Them things that go on land" was Cornelius Vanderbilt's dismissive term for railroads during the first 20 years or so of their existence in America. He had more reason than most people to be wary of them, having suffered two cracked ribs and a punctured lung in the world's first head-on crash, an 1833 mishap in New Jersey. Nor did Vanderbilt have any pressing financial reasons to invest in "them things." Starting with that $100 periauger, he had built an empire out of things that go on water.

"A coarse, tobacco-chewing, profane oaf of a man" was how railroad historian Aaron E. Klein once summed up Cornelius Vanderbilt, but that

The steamship C. Vanderbilt, *weighing over 1,000 tons, traveled at a top speed of 25 miles per hour.*
PHOTO © SHELBURNE MUSEUM, SHELBURNE, VERMONT.

description isn't that uncommon on the resumé of a New York entrepreneur in the first decades of the 19th century. What this particular oaf accomplished, by the age of 20, was the establishment of a regular passenger ferry service between Staten Island and Manhattan, followed by the securing of lucrative contracts to supply military posts around New York harbor during the War of 1812. Investing his profits in bigger vessels, he shouldered his way into the coastal trade linking New York, New England, and the South. By the late 1830s he was running one of America's largest fleets of steamboats, and had been christened "Commodore" by the newspapers.

In 1855 Vanderbilt introduced regular steamship service to Europe, and two years later he launched *Vanderbilt*, then the largest and fastest liner on the Atlantic. By that time he was 63, and rich enough to retire by the standards of any era. But in 1862, he started to buy stock in the New York and Harlem Railroad. He had the bug, and in only two years was out of steamships altogether. Abetted by $20 million in capital and the sheer force of will, he commenced the campaign that brought him control of the New York Central in 1867. At first, the Commodore was uncharacteristically content with command of the rails between New York and Buffalo—"if we take hold of roads running all the way to Chicago, we might as well go to San Francisco and to China," he told his son, William H. Vanderbilt. But the completion of the transcontinental railroad in 1869 convinced him that access to the rough new metropolis on Lake Michigan was a must for any Eastern railroad

that wanted to stay in business. The completion of the New York Central System between New York and Chicago was the Commodore's monument. So was the $100 million he amassed by the time of his death, in 1877, at the age of 82.

As far as more conventional monuments go, we might look to the statue of the Commodore that stands before New York's Grand Central Station, the hand extended as if this frock-coated gentleman is asking for a fare. But such an august apotheosis hardly does the wily boatman justice. He was a far livelier character than that bronze effigy suggests.

Was Cornelius Vanderbilt a coarse oaf? He certainly didn't have much schooling; he was too eager to get out on the water for that. He supposedly read only two books in his life, the Bible and Bunyan's *Pilgrim's Progress*. His grammar was bad and his command of profanity was impressive; he no doubt figured that what was good for the New York waterfront in 1810 was good for the world of high-stakes railroad finance in the 1860s—a conclusion in which he was probably not mistaken.

Still, the Commodore occasionally felt left out of refined society. The more genteel New York business figures, most of whom he could buy and sell by the time he reached middle age, left him out of their social circles, and he felt even more excluded from European society. "I've been to England, and seen them lords, and other fellows, and knew that I had twice as much brains as they had maybe," Vanderbilt once remarked, "and yet I had to keep still, and couldn't say anything for fear of exposing myself." Pangs of that sort turned the Commodore from a bluff disdain to a grudging respect for education, and no doubt helped lead to the million-dollar donation that helped turn struggling Central University, in Nashville, Tennessee, into Vanderbilt University.

What Vanderbilt lacked in erudition, he made up for in his physical presence and strength of will. He stood six foot one, had a leonine head and formidable sideburns, and retained the boatman's strength of his youth well past middle age. At the age of 50, he pummeled a champion boxer into near-insensibility during one of the era's no-holds-barred political

(OPPOSITE)

*Fifth Avenue was Vanderbilt territory in the
1880s. Far left, William H. Vanderbilt's home;
far right, William K.'s chateau.*

MUSEUM OF THE CITY OF NEW YORK.

(ABOVE)

*Mrs. Alva Smith Vanderbilt, mistress of Marble
House and a Fifth Avenue mansion. She later
married Oliver Belmont.*

PHOTO COURTESY THE PRESERVATION SOCIETY OF NEWPORT COUNTY.

Fast Trotters on Harlem Lane, N.Y. *John Cameron; colored lithograph; 1870. Cornelius Vanderbilt works his trotters on New York's Harlem Lane, as depicted by Currier and Ives.*

campaigns (Vanderbilt was a Whig; the boxer, who had threatened him, was a Tammany Hall Democrat). He was just as formidable when it came to using his financial muscle. Addressing a cabal of stock manipulators who had temporarily seized control of his Atlantic-to-Pacific transportation enterprise in Nicaragua, he wrote simply, "I won't sue you, for the law is too slow. I'll ruin you." And he did.

The Commodore could be a terrible bully, especially with his wife. When he insisted that the family move from their expansive Staten Island estate to a new house near Washington Square, in Manhattan's fashionable Greenwich Village, Sophia Vanderbilt balked to the point of becoming hysterical. Her husband's response was to commit her to a sanitarium, where she remained for two months. He also threw George Westinghouse bodily out of his office when the young man came to promote his new air brakes. But he could also be reasonable, in his crusty way. He was riding on one of his own trains one day when an employee, who didn't recognize him, told him to put out his cigar. Vanderbilt refused, and the man insisted— even after the Commodore identified himself. That impressed Vanderbilt, who commended the employee for upholding company rules no matter what.

The richest man in America took his pleasures modestly enough, although he wasn't averse to an occasional grand gesture such as building a steam yacht to carry himself, his family, and a few friends on a tour of Europe in 1853. But aside from playing whist with cronies and taking an occasional vacation at Saratoga Springs—his displeasure with some thick-cut fried

Red marble columns topped by bronze capitals flank the main dining room at The Breakers. The entire 70-room structure was built of stone, marble, and alabaster—Cornelius Vanderbilt II wanted no flammable materials used in construction.

Going to the Opera—A Family Portrait, *by Seymour Guy, 1873. The figures in the portrait are William Henry and Louisa Vanderbilt with seven of their eight sons and daughters, spouses or fiancees, and two servants. From left to right, they are: father William H., son Frederick, Mrs. William H., son George, daughter Florence, son William K., daughter Eliza, daughter Margaret, E. F. Shepard (Margaret's husband), servant, daughter Emily, servant, Alice Gwynne (Cornelius II's wife), W. Sloane (Emily's husband), son Cornelius II.*

Sophia Vanderbilt died in 1868. The following year, the Commodore married 30-year-old Frank Crawford, a distant relative whom he had met socially at Saratoga. The other eyebrow-raising indulgence of his last decade was an interest in spiritualism. Like most participants in the newly popular seances of that era, Vanderbilt wanted to contact the spirits of departed relatives, particularly his mother and a long-dead son. But being Cornelius Vanderbilt, he also looked to the world beyond for stock market tips.

Vanderbilt himself joined the inside traders of the choir invisible on January 4, 1877. The principal heir to that $100 million fortune was his son, William H. Vanderbilt, and along with the money went control of the New York Central. It was William H. who completed the Central's progression into Chicago, and otherwise put the road on the solid footing that would see it into the 20th century. Unfortunately for William's legacy, he was also the man who uttered the famous words, "The public be damned." There is good reason to believe that the remark, taken out of context, wasn't meant quite that way; but the damage was done. On the eve of the muckraking era it seemed an impolitic sentiment, coming from a big fat man with cartoon-quality muttonchops, a pair of Fifth Avenue townhouses, and a prize racehorse pastured on a piece of midtown Manhattan real estate in sight of the executive offices at the original Grand Central Terminal.

William H. Vanderbilt died in 1885, and after that the Vanderbilts served mostly as directors of the New York Central; within a generation or two, they were

potatoes at a hotel there is supposed to have led to the invention of potato chips—his favorite pastime was harness racing. Vanderbilt drove his own handsome pair of trotters alone to his lower Manhattan office each day, and in his leisure hours he became such a figure on the suburban roads where fashionable horsemen gathered that he and his equipage were depicted by Currier and Ives. The Commodore stoked himself for the day's activities with his favorite breakfast of three lamb chops and eight egg yolks right up to his eighties. His constitution was so strong that for him, the white of the egg was the part you threw away.

absent from the corporate structure. What they did do,
especially in the generation represented by William H.'s
sons, was build houses. Fifth Avenue was filled with
these now-vanished extravaganzas, especially along the
blocks between Fifty-first and Fifty-eighth streets.
William K. Vanderbilt put up an immense turreted
chateau, and his son built another right next door. Just
up the street was Cornelius II's castle, done in the style
of a chateau on the Loire and big enough to have served
as the Central's main terminal. Cornelius II's greatest
extravagance, though, was The Breakers, his "cottage"
in Newport, Rhode Island. Designed by Richard
Morris Hunt in the style of a Genoese palace of the
17th century, its interior gilt to a fare-thee-well and its
grounds landscaped by Frederick Law Olmsted, the
70-room Breakers surpasses even William K.
Vanderbilt, Sr.'s nearby Marble House as the most
extravagant of Newport's turn-of-the-century mansions.
The Breakers would cost an estimated $400 million—
four times the Commodore's entire legacy—to build
today, assuming one could find the materials and the
skilled manpower (2,500 workers, in those days before
power tools) to put them together.

But George Washington Vanderbilt III, youngest
son of William H., topped even The Breakers. In the
early 1890s, he created Biltmore House, a 250-room
confection modeled on the French chateaux of
Chambord, Chenonceaux, and Blois and set on 125,000
acres outside Asheville, North Carolina. It is the largest
private house ever constructed in America, and it still
remains in the family. But what began as the fiefdom of
a rather shy Vanderbilt interested in experimental forest

(OPPOSITE)

The Gothic Room at Marble House was one of several rooms featuring Alva's favorite styles — this time with French Gothic arches, chimney piece, ribbing, and figurative carving. The room originally held a collection of medieval art objects. William K. Vanderbilt spent $11 million on his Newport home.

PHOTO © RICHARD CHEEK FOR THE PRESERVATION SOCIETY OF NEWPORT COUNTY.

(ABOVE)

Alva Smith Belmont (formerly Vanderbilt) frequently entertained in her Chinese tea house, built in 1914 on the grounds of Marble House. A lavish Chinese costume ball heralded the opening of this delightful tea house. Originally standing directly above the Cliff Walk, overlooking the Atlantic, the structure was moved back from the edge when the seawall weakened, threatening to send the small, colorful pavilion adrift.

PHOTO © RICHARD CHEEK FOR THE PRESERVATION SOCIETY OF NEWPORT COUNTY.

(ABOVE)

Frederick W. Vanderbilt's Rough Point
(eventually owned by tobacco heiress Doris Duke)
succeeded somewhat better than most Newport
"cottages" at harmonizing with the landscape.
Here we see it on a typical New England overcast
summer day.

PHOTO NEWPORT RESTORATION FOUNDATION, NEWPORT, RHODE
ISLAND.

(RIGHT)

The solarium at Rough Point: Airiness and
ornament somehow coexist, with a grand Atlantic
vista beyond.

PHOTO NEWPORT RESTORATION FOUNDATION, NEWPORT, RHODE
ISLAND.

The grand staircase landing at Rough Point, complete with large portraits, is lighted by large windows on the landing featuring stained-glass coats of arms.

PHOTO NEWPORT RESTORATION FOUNDATION, NEWPORT, RHODE ISLAND.

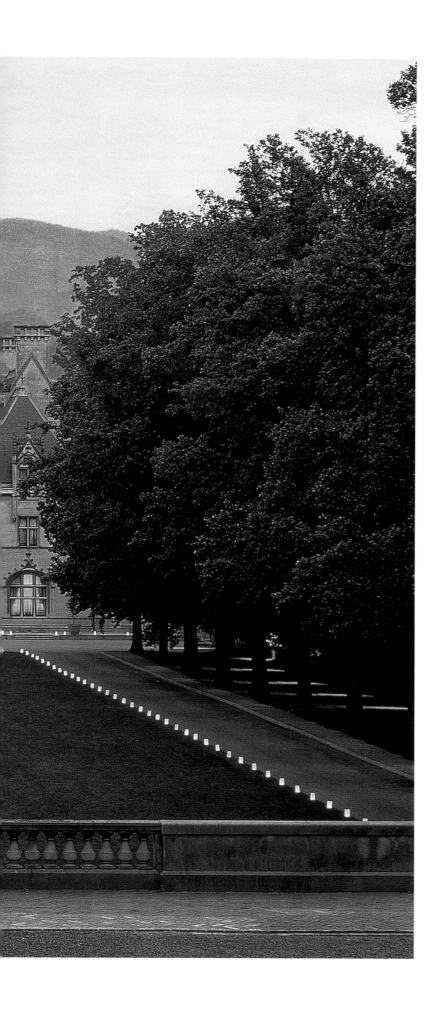

practices is now a major tourist attraction, its surrounding acreage diminished to 7,000 acres.

G. W. Vanderbilt was one of the most earnest and intriguing members of a family that produced a generous share of what society editors used to call "sportsmen." He never went near the railroad business, and seems to have been the first Vanderbilt to realize that inherited wealth (his own legacy amounted to $10 million) might be used to finance a life of study as well as conspicuous consumption. To build a 250-room house is, no doubt, to consume rather conspicuously. But G.W. Vanderbilt took a far more than superficial interest in the development of his estate.

Only 27 when he began to buy his North Carolina acreage, Vanderbilt hired two men who were at the peak of their professions: Richard Morris Hunt as architect, and Frederick Law Olmsted as landscape designer. Unlike many Gilded Age nabobs who were difficult if not impossible patrons, Vanderbilt impressed both Hunt and Olmsted with his sincere interest in their work. "Affectionate solicitude" was the phrase Hunt's wife used to describe his attitude toward Hunt; while Olmsted, in a letter to his landscape architect son, referred to the Vanderbilt commission as a "school" in which a great deal could be learned.

As much as he enjoyed architecture and garden design, G.W. Vanderbilt reserved his greatest enthusiasm for his forests. He hired Gifford Pinchot, father of the U.S. Forest Service, to manage his woodlands. Later, the job fell to

pioneer silviculturist Carl A. Schenck, who founded the Biltmore Forest School. The legacy of modern forestry education, and of the Pisgah National Forest, which comprises much of the original estate, are the most important contributions of a Vanderbilt who, retiring as he was, couldn't have retired to more splendid surroundings.

RAILROAD GIANTS

There were two kinds of railroad men operating in what historian Oliver Jensen has called "the age of bare knuckles." There were the builders and consolidators, men like the Vanderbilts who either created railroad companies and laid track, or at least did a reasonable job of managing roads they had acquired through mergers and takeovers. Then there were the outright scalawags, men whose main interest was the manipulation of railroad stock and the squeezing of value from roads that might well be turned into barren husks by the time the opportunists were finished. "I don't build railroads, I buy them," said Jay Gould, the most notorious exemplar of the latter modus operandi. Both the builders and the manipulators, though, fought with bare knuckles.

One of the great builders was a man remembered to this day in the name of the Amtrak train that runs between Chicago and Seattle. The *Empire Builder* follows the northernmost of the major U.S. rail routes, coursing across the high prairie that reaches from Minnesota's Twin Cities to the foothills of the Rocky Mountains, then traverses both the Rockies and the Cascades before its descent to Puget Sound.

(OPPOSITE)

Biltmore's rich-textured libary is home to more
than 10,000 volumes selected from George
Vanderbilt's personal collection of 23,000 books.
A 17th-century tapestry above the black marble
fireplace is flanked by walnut figures of Hestia
(goddess of the hearth), and Demeter (goddess of
the earth) carved by Karl Bitter.

PHOTO USED WITH PERMISSION FROM THE BILMORE COMPANY,
ASHEVILLE, NORTH CAROLINA.

(ABOVE)

Biltmore's banquet hall, the largest and most
dramatic room of the house, features a 72-foot
ceiling, triple fireplace, and 16th-century
Brussels tapestries.

PHOTO USED WITH PERMISSION FROM THE BILTMORE COMPANY,
ASHEVILLE, NORTH CAROLINA.

(ABOVE)

A salon in the Stanford White–designed Hyde Park, New York, home of Frederick W. Vanderbilt, completed in 1899.

(RIGHT)

The largest of the two dining tables in Hyde Park's massive dining room can seat 30 people and was used for formal affairs. The smaller table was used when the Frederick Vanderbilts dined alone.

(ABOVE)

The picture of propriety: one of Newport's prominent citizens out for an afternoon ride in a spotless carriage pulled by a proud and impeccably groomed horse.

PHOTO COURTESY THE PRESERVATION SOCIETY OF NEWPORT COUNTY.

(LEFT)

Winters along the New England coast are typically cold and damp, but Newport society always found ways to enjoy the outdoors.

PHOTO COURTESY THE PRESERVATION SOCIETY OF NEWPORT COUNTY.

(OPPOSITE)

From head to toe this Newport family is appropriately attired and prepares to receive guests at an afternoon garden party.

PHOTO COURTESY THE PRESERVATION SOCIETY OF NEWPORT COUNTY.

(OPPOSITE TOP)

With coachmen standing by, spectators enjoy a turn-of-the-century Newport regatta.

PHOTO COURTESY THE NEWPORT HISTORICAL SOCIETY.

(OPPOSITE BOTTOM)

Newport summer sojourners stage a "mattress race" with inflatable rafts on Bailey's Beach, 1921.

PHOTO COURTESY THE NEWPORT HISTORICAL SOCIETY.

(ABOVE)

The Vanderbilts enjoy an afternoon outing on their yacht.

PHOTO BY HENRY O. HAVERMEYER COURTESY THE PRESERVATION SOCIETY OF NEWPORT COUNTY.

(ABOVE)

*A Vanderbilt family safari in Africa. Alva, still a
Vanderbilt at the time of the photo, lounges in the
hammock at right.*

PHOTO COURTESY THE PRESERVATION SOCIETY OF NEWPORT COUNTY.

(OPPOSITE)

*A summer afternoon crowd turns out for a tennis
match at the Casino, Newport.*

PHOTO BY HENRY O. HAVERMEYER/COURTESY THE NEWPORT
HISTORICAL SOCIETY.

(ABOVE)

Then as now, Newport's Cliff Walk drew summer strollers, c. 1910. The Breakers stands in the background.

PHOTO COURTESY THE NEWPORT HISTORICAL SOCIETY.

(LEFT)

A summer fete on the lawn at The Breakers, probably during the first decade of the 20th century.

PHOTO COURTESY THE NEWPORT HISTORICAL SOCIETY.

The Empire Builder himself was an émigré from Ontario named James Jerome Hill. His creation was the Great Northern Railway.

Jim Hill had wanted to become a doctor, but he gave up that ambition after losing an eye in a boyhood accident. When he was 18, in 1856, he drifted down to St. Paul, Minnesota, where he hoped to join a fur-trading expedition. But he missed the company's departure, and instead settled down to clerking for a steamboat outfit. By 1865 he was working for himself, forwarding freight and running a warehouse. As a

sideline, he got into the coal business. His assumption was that coal would soon replace wood as locomotive fuel, and that there would be plenty of locomotives to burn it.

Hill's next move was to assume a partnership in the Red River Transportation Company, which ran steamships north to a Canadian settlement called Fort Garry, soon to be renamed Winnipeg. In 1878, he and his partners bought the bankrupt St. Paul and Pacific Railroad, one of Hill's old freight clients. Savvy St. Paul businessmen figured Hill was buying nothing but

trouble, because his new acquisition was a poorly built road that served a farming district beset by grasshoppers and depression. But things began to pick up just as Hill was linking up with the lines north of the border, and in 1879 he reorganized the firm as the St. Paul, Minneapolis, and Manitoba.

Hill, by now fully in charge of his road, began planning his next move. It was a scheme that struck the sober citizens of St. Paul as particularly hare-brained, and quickly earned the label "Hill's Folly": James J. Hill was going to run the St. P M&M clear across the Dakotas and Montana, across Idaho and Washington, straight to Puget Sound.

It took until 1893, but Hill pulled it off. His railroad—known after 1883 as the Great Northern Railway—not only spanned the northernmost U.S. route, but the job had been accomplished without any of the federal land grants that had eased the way for other builders of transcontinental lines. Later, Hill also took control of the Northern Pacific and the Chicago, Burlington and Quincy. The Empire Builder had done his job.

Perhaps no other railroad man was as intimately involved in creating the economy and social structure of the territory his lines traversed as was James J. Hill. He advertised for settlers to populate the prairie, distributing seeds and fertilizer, livestock, and the latest information on husbandry and agronomy to the farmers who put their roots down along the Great Northern tracks. (Later, after the region fought its way through drought and hard times, many would say that Hill had overpopulated the high plains.) He was also a wizard at creating complementary shipping patterns, juggling

midwestern wheat, Pacific Northwest lumber, and southern cotton bound for the Orient so that his trains were always making money.

So were Hill's other investments. He once took a flier on a remote chunk of real estate in northern Minnesota, which unbeknownst to buyer or seller contained the Mesabi iron range. He leased the property to U.S. Steel, reaping abundant profits for himself and the Great Northern's stockholders.

With his barrel chest, wiry gray beard, and one good eye that seemed to burn the more fiercely for the

One of the many gas-fired hearths (in summer dress) at the James J. Hill House, St. Paul.

absence of the other, Jim Hill was the picture of the crusty capitalist warhorse of the late 19th century. He acted the part, too—if an isolated prairie town eager for a Great Northern connection refused to meet his terms, he would consign it to obscurity by stranding it off the main line. But Hill had a solid respect for men willing to work as hard as he was. On at least one occasion he rode his private car out into the deep prairie snows, then picked up a shovel and put his shoulder to the work while the men he relieved rested and drank coffee in his plush parlor on wheels.

James J. Hill built things big, and he built them solid. Tracks, bridges, rolling stock, locomotives—all were the best he could afford. On Summit Avenue in St. Paul, his massive stone mansion speaks to the same desire to build for the ages. It isn't a cozy house, though we can be sure it was warm enough: its behemoth boilers gobbled enough coal each winter to send a fleet of freight trains across the prairie, and most rooms were equipped with gas fireplaces. The music room with its huge built-in pipe organ seems like a small concert hall, and the dining room like a school refectory; and even giving allowance for its present-day status as a tourist attraction, the halls have a dour institutional feel. But there is one relatively snug room where the spirit of the builder breathes. It isn't difficult to imagine Jim Hill in his office, plotting his next art acquisitions (oddly, he favored modern French painters rather than the safe academicians most rich men went for in his day), planning his quiet bequests to Catholic charities . . . and musing, in the last years before his death in 1916,

on how a one-eyed boy from Ontario might see an iron road to Seattle beginning on the wharves of St. Paul.

The Great Northern was, of course, not the first railroad to traverse the western vastnesses of North America. The Northern Pacific had finished its 14-year task of linking the Great Lakes with the Columbia River valley in 1883, largely due to the organizational genius of a German immigrant named Henry Villard. Villard was, perhaps, the unlikeliest of railroad titans. He first turned up in the United States in 1853, when he was 18. Starting with menial jobs (one was on a railroad crew), the university-trained Villard became a newspaperman and a respected Civil War correspondent. He promoted civil service reform, and married the daughter of the uncompromising New England abolitionist William Lloyd Garrison (their son, Oswald Garrison Villard, would carry on the family's progressive traditions as editor of *The Nation*). But in the early 1870s, Villard returned to Germany to nurse chronic health problems.

Villard's 1874 return to the United States was prompted by a group of German investors, who wanted him to keep an eye on a couple of ailing western railroads in which they held stock. Within a few years, he became president of the Oregon and California and a receiver of the Kansas Pacific. Seeing that the biggest threat to his companies' position in the Northwest market was the still-incomplete Northern Pacific, Villard in 1881 made a bold decision: he would buy the competing line. His

means of financing the acquisition, though, would be even bolder.

Villard approached 50 wealthy Americans, most of whom he knew personally from his years in the U.S., and who knew him as a man of integrity. He asked them to finance an $8 million fund he was amassing for a purpose he could not yet disclose. This was the soon-to-be-legendary "Blind Pool," eventually totaling $12 million, which enabled Villard to purchase the Northern Pacific on behalf of his trusting investors. Installing himself as president, he marshaled the men and material

needed to finish the NP's route to the west coast by 1883.

Ousted as president of the NP and later returned in the role of chairman, Villard in later life pursued interests that ranged far beyond railroads. He bought the *New York Evening Post*, helped organize the Edison General Electric Company, and electrified Milwaukee's street railway system. He represented Deutsche Bank in the U.S., and gave generously to the universities of Washington and Oregon. Although a relatively modest man by railroad baron standards, he also made a

The last word in travel comfort, 1895: Interior of the private railroad car Grand Isle .
PHOTO © SHELBURNE MUSEUM, SHELBURNE, VERMONT.

significant addition to the midtown Manhattan streetscape. The "Villard Houses," as they came to be called, were built between 1882 and 1886 on Madison Avenue between East 50th and East 51st streets. Villard lived in only one of the four Italian Renaissance-style houses, which were designed by McKim, Mead & White (with a later addition by Babb, Cook & Willard) to give the impression of a single palatial edifice embracing a front courtyard. The railroad man sold the other units to friends.

The Villard houses would later be divided between the Roman Catholic Archdiocese of New York and the publishing firm of Random House. Eventually, they faced demolition—but the luxury hotel that was to replace them was instead integrated into the block, so that the houses' façades and a portion of their interior now welcome hotel guests. "Façadomy," some critics call this sort of preservation, but it beats the alternative. Henry Villard himself was a man who appreciated creative approaches to a problem.

The most celebrated of all transcontinental rail routes was the first to have been completed, when the crews of the Union Pacific and Central Pacific met at Promontory Point, Utah, for the driving of the last spike in 1869. The Union Pacific spent much of the next several decades mired in scandal and bankruptcy, eventually becoming the "streak of rust" purchased and rehabilitated by E. H. Harriman, whom we'll meet later on. It was the Central Pacific that produced the legendary team of eyes-on-the-main-chance entrepreneurs known collectively as the Big Four: Leland Stanford, Mark Hopkins, Charles Crocker, and Collis P. Huntington.

They were only a medium-sized four, to begin with. Shopkeepers all, they were easterners who had decamped for California in the wake of the 1849 gold rush. Being men of good sense, they left the actual mining to others and went in for more of a sure thing, staying put in Sacramento and operating on the theory that regardless of whether or not a man found gold, he needed to buy pants, food, and a shovel. Huntington and Hopkins sold hardware; Crocker and his brother owned three dry goods stores; Stanford, who helped found the California Republican Party in 1852, was in the grocery business.

These four merchants were on hand at a meeting in Sacramento one day in 1861 to hear a visionary named Theodore Judah, known as "Crazy" Judah for his fanatical devotion to his cause, lay out his plan for a railroad across the Sierra Nevada—part of an eventual transcontinental route he had been promoting since the early 1850s. Huntington, Hopkins, Crocker, and Stanford didn't think Judah was crazy. They bought enough stock in his scheme to guarantee that it would get off the ground, got the U.S. government to pass the Pacific Railroad Act in 1862, and started construction at Sacramento in January 1863. Along the way they bought out Theodore Judah's share of the Central Pacific, as the new enterprise was called, for $100,000. Judah died shortly afterward, while heading east to find backers to help *him* buy out the Big Four.

But those four erstwhile Sacramento storekeepers held on to the operation, using every trick in the book to get their road built and make the greatest possible amount of money doing it. A firm set up by Crocker

got the construction contract, and the Central Pacific secured the bigger government loans earmarked for mountainous terrain by claiming that the level ground on which tracklaying began was actually in the rugged Sierra foothills. Eventually, the company evolved into the Southern Pacific, a titan of western transportation so formidable that it was the thinly veiled model for the voracious rail colossus in Frank Norris's muckraking classic *The Octopus*.

As partners go, the masterminds of the Central Pacific couldn't have been more different. Stanford, originally a lawyer, was the most gregarious of the four and a born politician—he served a term as governor of California (1862–1864) and was a U.S. senator from 1885 to 1893, representing his railroad as faithfully as he did his state . . . or more so. Along with the limelight, Stanford loved the good life. He owned a palatial private railroad car, bred prize racehorses at his Palo Alto ranch, and cultivated extensive vineyards. His mansion on San Francisco's Nob Hill was the height of overstuffed Victorian splendor.

Charles Crocker was the man who promoted the

William Van Horne's now-vanished Montreal mansion was a 52-room treasury of paintings, tapestries, and Japanese pottery.
PHOTO CANADIAN PACIFIC RAILWAY ARCHIVES, MONTREAL.

idea of using Chinese labor to build the Central Pacific. His rationale was simple: "They built the Great Wall, didn't they?" Crocker was the field boss of the operation, swaggering up and down the line, all 250 pounds of him, bullying the rails into place and doling out silver and gold coins himself on payday. He had a showy San Francisco mansion, too. One of its notable features was a 40-foot-high spite fence, built around the modest home of the only property owner on his block who refused to sell out.

Mark Hopkins would have been happy with that man's cottage. He was an accountant by training and inclination, and a cheapskate by nature. The only reason "Uncle Mark" ended up in a Nob Hill palace was that his wife insisted on it. His greatest pleasure seemed to have been keeping the railroad's books, and he would no doubt have shaken his head in disapproval at the luxuriousness of the San Francisco hotel that bears his name today.

"Ruthless as a crocodile," "no more soul than a shark." Those were just a few of the phrases used to describe Collis P. Huntington during his heyday as biggest of the Big Four; in retaliation, Huntington called the organized farmers of the Grange movement "Communists." The bald, stocky, white-bearded Huntington honed his pragmatic ruthlessness as he elbowed his way in line for hard-to-come-by construction supplies during the Civil War, and dipped into company slush funds for purposes of legislative persuasion. He never cared for the limelight—he was happy to have Stanford be the Central Pacific president and chief mouthpiece—and despite his Western

notoriety among the Grangers and other anti-monopolists, he alone among the Big Four became primarily a resident of the East. That was where the brains of the Central/Southern Pacific operation could best keep an eye on Wall Street, and on his other interests. When John D. Rockefeller, Sr., moved to New York, his first home was a lavishly furnished brownstone where Huntington had lately installed his mistress.

The San Francisco earthquake of 1906 erased the mansions of the three lifelong Californians among the Big Four, but one monument (aside from their railroad) remains: Stanford University, officially Leland Stanford, Jr., University, created by Stanford in 1885 in memory of his late son.

WILLIAM CORNELIUS VAN HORNE

"Oh, I eat all I can, I drink all I can, I smoke all I can, and I don't give a damn about anything."

The words of an idle sybarite? Not exactly. He may have worked hard at enjoying his creature comforts, but William Cornelius Van Horne worked harder at getting things done. He was an accomplished telegrapher, bookkeeper, art collector, amateur painter, gentleman farmer, and discoverer of nine fossils which bear the designation *van hornei*. And he built the Canadian Pacific Railway.

It's one of the ironies of North American railroad history that while James J. Hill, builder of the Great Northern, was an Ontario boy, William Van Horne was an Illinois native who earned his fame—and a knighthood—in Canada. Alone among the great names

of railroading on this continent, Van Horne acquired his reputation not as a financier, but as a manager. Born in 1843, he had by age 38 worked his way up to the presidency of the Southern Minnesota Railway after starting out as a telegrapher with the Illinois Central. In 1881, when the Canadian Pacific Railway was chartered by an act of Canada's parliament, Van Horne was recommended for the job of general manager by none other than Jim Hill, a member of the CPR syndicate (the two men later became bitter enemies when Van Horne successfully opposed Hill's plan to run

the CPR south of the Great Lakes, where it would be a feeder line for his roads).

Managing the CPR meant building the bulk of the road from scratch, and marshaling the men and materials for this gigantic task revealed Van Horne's genius. During the 10 years preceding his appointment, the Canadian government and its various franchisees had laid only 300 miles of track. In 1882, Van Horne's crews extended the CPR 418 miles through the prairie provinces in 10 *months*. The going was a good deal slower across the stubborn rock and muskeg north of

(ABOVE)

A windmill at Covenhoven. William Van Horne
was equally fascinated by art and technology, and
was adept at both.

PHOTO CANADIAN PACIFIC RAILWAY ARCHIVES, MONTREAL.

(LEFT)

William Van Horne's summer home Covenhoven,
on Minister's Island in New Brunswick: it took
eight men to lift the living room rug.

PHOTO CANADIAN PACIFIC RAILWAY ARCHIVES, MONTREAL.

Lake Superior, and in the steep passes of the Rocky Mountains. But Van Horne got the job done, and stood among the laborers and dignitaries that gathered on November 7, 1885, at a remote spot called Craigellachie in British Columbia. At that last spike ceremony, the general manager was modest and sparing in his remarks: "All I can say is that the work has been done well in every way." A tremendous share of that work had been done by the general manager himself, a man unafraid to take the throttle of a locomotive and run the machine over a new high trestle, after the engineer had looked down and lost his nerve.

Van Horne—Sir William Cornelius Van Horne after 1894—became president of the CPR in 1888, and board chairman 11 years later. Those were the years when the stout, bald, elegantly bearded railroader commanded his empire of trains, steamships, and luxury hotels (several of which he had helped design) from his office in Montreal's Windsor Station, and when he might be seen just about anywhere along the CPR lines in his splendid private car *Saskatchewan*, crafted of mahogany and glittering with polished brass. Home for Van Horne was a baronial 52-room stone mansion in Montreal, its walls hung with a $3 million collection of Old Masters, but in summer Sir William would likely be found at his island farm near St. Andrews, New Brunswick. There he plunged into landscaping and agricultural tasks, plotting out vineyards, orchards, greenhouses, and stables. He expected everyone to work as hard as he did: when he found a group of his dairymen idly looking out of a barn window, he sent a team of carpenters to raise the window above eye level.

Lyndhurst in the Hudson Valley darkness. Jay Gould's redoubt is now a National Trust property.

During his last days, in 1915, his doctors had told him not to smoke more than three cigars a day. He followed their orders scrupulously . . . but only after ordering a box of two-foot cigars that would last four hours apiece. Whatever was worth doing, the genius of the CPR figured, was worth doing on a colossal scale.

JAY GOULD

If William Van Horne represented one end of the spectrum of constructive toil during railroading's great era of expansion, there was no shortage of out-and-out rascals at the other end. The most notorious of this crew could be found, toward the latter part of his life, nursing his dyspepsia at his romantic Gothic mansion, Lyndhurst, on the banks of the Hudson in Tarrytown, New York. But there was nothing romantic about Jay Gould. Born in modest circumstances in upstate New York in 1836, he worked as a tanner in Pennsylvania and honed his business skills as a leather merchant in pre–Civil War New York City. Around that time he began speculating in railroad securities, living out his later self-description as a buyer, not a builder, of railroads. His career as a manipulator led to his eventual involvement with the most star-crossed road of his day, the Erie. "The Scarlet Woman of Wall Street," that hapless firm was called, and it certainly had some colorful suitors.

The "Erie Wars" of the 1860s would fill a volume all their own. Suffice it to say that the railroad was the prize in a brazen game played by Gould along with two equally rapacious colleagues named Daniel Drew and James Fisk. At various junctures, the game involved

the issuing of fraudulent stock, the bribing of members of the New York State Legislature, and that extremely rare occurrence, the fleecing of one Commodore Cornelius Vanderbilt. When the dust settled, Vanderbilt had withdrawn in a compromise, Drew was ruined, Fisk was dead, and Gould left the field without the ravished Erie but with $25 million with which to play havoc among the western railroads. (Along the way, he had created the

financial panic called "Black Friday"—September 24,
1869—when he tried to corner the gold market.)

Although they were both pirates at heart, it's hard to
imagine two more different operators than Daniel Drew
and Jim Fisk. Drew, the Commodore's sometime whist
partner, was a rustic Vermonter who had once been a
cattle drover. The Wall Street term "watered stock,"
meaning stock inflated beyond its legitimate value, is
said to derive from a practice "Uncle Dan'l" perfected
when he was young: letting cattle lick salt and then
drink copiously just before delivering them to market,
so that he would make more money when he sold them
by weight. Like Vanderbilt, he had graduated to
railroads via steamboats, although you would never
catch him building his own steam yacht. Drew was a
lifelong cheapskate, who wore threadbare suits and ate
sandwiches at Delmonico's lunch counter while his
fellow buccaneers dined on lobster and canvasback
duck upstairs. He always carried a Bible, and he said
grace over the sandwiches.

"Jubilee Jim" Fisk was another Vermont boy made
good—or, more to the point, spectacularly bad. Unlike
Drew, he flaunted every dollar he earned or stole, right
down to wearing a custom-designed "admiral's" uniform
when riding in state on one of the steamboats he
wrested from Uncle Dan'l in the Erie Wars. ("If
Vanderbilt's a Commodore," he claimed, "I can be an
Admiral.") Plump and mustachioed, Fisk was very
much the ladies' man, and his favorite mistress was an
actress named Josie Mansfield. She was his undoing.
On January 6, 1872, Jubilee Jim was shot dead at the
Grand Central Hotel in New York by Edward Stokes,

Jay Gould's dining room at Lyndhurst. Chronically dyspeptic, the financier must have enjoyed the decor more than the meals.

The Great Hall of Arden House, last home of Edward H. Harriman.

another of Josie's admirers. He would have loved his own funeral, a spectacularly gaudy affair organized by his politician friends at Tammany Hall.

And Jay Gould? When he wasn't in seclusion at Lyndhurst, the frail little man with the big black beard might be found at his Fifth Avenue mansion, surrounded by fresh flowers from his Tarrytown greenhouses. That is, if anyone wanted to find him: in the words of a contemporary account, "He has few friends, and is suspicious of all his associates, who return his distrust with equal heartiness." He was once beaten by a Wall Street mob. He owned the New York *World* newspaper, and controlled the Western Union Telegraph Company. His digestion bothered him constantly, and he died, in 1892, at the age of 56.

His daughter, Anna, became the Duchess of Talleyrand-Perigord.

EDWARD HENRY HARRIMAN

Mention the name Harriman today, and anyone versed in 20th-century American politics will recall W. Averill Harriman, the suave, urbane New York State governor and ambassador. People living in the New York metropolitan area might also think of vast Harriman State Park, a component of the Palisades Interstate Park system just north of the New Jersey border. A hundred years ago, though, the name Harriman meant railroads.

The father of both the politician and the park was a small, steely-eyed man with an outsized walrus mustache named Edward Henry Harriman. To him belongs the distinction of controlling more miles of

track than any individual in the history of American railroading. He was neither a builder nor a buccaneer; rather, he combined the boldness and timing of a successful financier with the skills of a master administrator. Having seen the vultures pick the bones of many an unfortunate road, Harriman thought not in terms of overnight profits but of capital improvements that would lead to dependable long-term yields.

E. H. Harriman was born a minister's son in 1848. Leaving school for a job as a Wall Street office boy at 14, he borrowed $3,000 from an uncle and bought a seat on the New York Stock Exchange just seven years later. His introduction to railroad management was a directorship with a small, upstate New York road owned by his father-in-law; by the mid-1880s, he was instrumental in revitalizing the Illinois Central, and doubling that company's earnings.

Harriman hit his stride in 1894, when he led a syndicate that bought a railroad that had been dismissed by J. P. Morgan as "a streak of rust" when it went on the block after going bankrupt the previous year. The Union Pacific, partner with the Central Pacific in spanning the continent in 1869, had since been bled dry by Jay Gould and came in at a bargain price. Harriman, with his genius for management, doubled the UP's earnings within two years, while cutting its freight rates and vastly improving roadbeds and equipment. Next Harriman bought the Central and Southern Pacific railroads, following Collis P. Huntington's death in 1900. He was a director of the Santa Fe and the Erie. With these and a slew of other roads under his ownership or de facto control,

Harriman at his zenith was master of 60,000 to 65,000 miles of track, with another 35,000 miles of steamship lines thrown in. At a 1906 Interstate Commerce Commission hearing, he freely admitted that if there were no antitrust laws to stop him, he would keep buying railroads "as long as I live."

Although Harriman didn't live that much longer—he died in 1909—conservationists might well have wished that he could have kept buying land, as well. Keenly interested in saving forests from exploitation, Harriman acquired 20,000 acres in the Ramapo Mountains of southern New York, and crowned them with his one great extravagance, a 150-room French Renaissance mansion surrounded by formal gardens. Leaving Arden House and the surrounding property to his wife, Mary, along with his $100 million fortune, Harriman stipulated that 10,000 acres be given to the state for use as a park. His other accomplishments outside the realm of pure moneymaking included the adoption of the first pension plan for railroad workers, organization of a relief program for San Francisco following the 1906 earthquake, a flood protection plan for California's

Imperial Valley, and the organization of a scientific expedition to Alaska in 1899. He also left a vastly more efficient American rail system, an achievement which, he might have argued, earned him the right to a dollar or two, or a hundred million, in compensation.

There had been one big disappointment in E. H. Harriman's career. That was his failure to obtain control of the Northern Pacific Railroad, which he had hoped to snatch from under the nose of James J. Hill. The scheme involved the purchase of an outstanding 40,000 shares of Northern Pacific stock, and might have succeeded if a less sensitive nose had been involved. As it was, Hill got hold of those shares before Harriman did, thus cementing what had been his minority control of Henry Villard's old road. Hill's purchase of the NP stock was executed by his New York bankers, partners in a firm whose chairman was in France on one of his frequent art-buying sprees. The partners cabled their boss, who gave his approval to the deal and presumably did not mind being interrupted by the affairs of so important a client as Hill. The banker was John Pierpont Morgan.

J. P. MORGAN

No farmboy, frontier trader, or scion of a small-town preacher, J. P. Morgan was comfortable from birth. The man who rose to become America's master banker never had to worry, as did Astor or Vanderbilt, about fitting in with polite society. As art dealer James Duveen observed, "Morgan was born a gentleman, and did everything he could to fortify that fact and impose it upon an admiring world."

Morgan entered the admiring world in 1837, born into a Hartford, Connecticut, family that had done well in retailing, real estate, and insurance, and was about to do even better in banking. Pierpont's father, Junius Spencer Morgan, became a key figure in the movement of British venture capital to America's growing railroads, and by the time the boy was 20 he was accustomed to transatlantic travel, had studied in Switzerland and Germany, and was beginning to take a hand in his father's enterprises.

For a man whose very name came to signify total control, and absolute mastery of every situation he encountered, it is interesting to note that J. P. Morgan was, for the first 53 years of his life, subsidiary to his father in the older man's banking business. But Junius gave his son an ever-increasing amount of leeway during the boom years following the Civil War, and J. P. Morgan knew what to do with it. He became increasingly involved with the growing railroads, parlaying his role as investment banker into a string of strategic directorships and eventually outright control of a number of major roads. He also backed new technology, becoming an early investor in Thomas Edison's fledgling company as well as one of the first New York customers for Edison's electric lighting apparatus.

By middle age, J. P. Morgan had become one of those individuals who dominates his peers and his surroundings not only by cleverness and will, but by sheer physical presence. Morgan was average in height but weighed a bullish 210 pounds; he had an enormous head, commanding brow, and eyes that reminded the young photographer Edward Steichen of the headlights of a locomotive bearing down on whomever was in their sight. His one physical disfigurement—a nose turned hideous and bulbous by acne rosacea—was at first a cause for shyness and self-consciousness, but came to be a lantern flashed in defiance at the world.

The peak of J. P. Morgan's power and fame coincided with the last quarter-century of his life. From 1890 until his death in 1913, Morgan, for better or worse, represented the power of centralized finance in

the United States. His passion was for organization, and reorganization. With the railroads hauled out of the chaos of the wide-open heyday of the Goulds and Drews, Morgan turned to the steel industry, consolidating the Carnegie, Frick, and other competing firms into U.S. Steel, the nation's first billion-dollar company. (In 1901, a billion dollars represented 4 percent of the national wealth of the United States.) The other accomplishment for which Morgan is most widely remembered is his role in the Panic of 1907, putting together a coalition of banks willing to commit

their resources to halt a cascade of bank failures that threatened the nation's economy. This was the last time, in those days before the creation of the Federal reserve system, that a private citizen would (or could) assume such a leadership position.

Morgan may have been a private citizen, but he lived like a Renaissance doge. His image was perhaps enhanced by the fact that unlike financial titans who view conspicuous consumption as a badge of celebrity (or even as the vehicle for their celebrity), Morgan gave the appearance of a man whose appetites existed in and of themselves, and would be every bit as grand even if no publicity were to accrue to them. "As long as he was in active life, and in whatever field he entered, he bought the highest-priced corner lot," wrote his son-in-law and biographer Herbert Satterlee. "He added championship horses to his stable, built the best steam yacht, and purchased the most notable pictures."

That summed up Morgan's magnificence, as much as anything. Like most of his fabulously wealthy contemporaries, J. P. Morgan lived on a lavish personal scale: He employed a succession of four splendid yachts, all named *Corsair*, to ferry friends and business associates up the Hudson from New York to his riverside country house, Cragston. He was commodore of the New York Yacht Club. He bred prize collies and cattle, had his gargantuan cigars custom-made in Cuba from select-harvest tobacco, and ate eight-course breakfasts. "Always resist everything except temptation," he once told an associate, and his Lucullan appetites extended to some of the most beautiful women of the age, whom he entertained in those off hours when

he wasn't singing hymns with Episcopalian bishops. But "the most notable pictures," and a collection of equally notable manuscripts and books, were Morgan's greatest extravagance.

Starting humbly enough at age 14 with President Millard Fillmore's autograph, Morgan went on to collect shards of medieval stained glass in towns he visited as a student in Europe; later, he graduated to ancient Egyptian pieces. But his ambitions as a grand acquisitor really burst forth after the death of his father, when he became known among transatlantic art dealers

as a man who would swallow entire collections, and outbid anyone for anything.

Morgan bought Chinese ceramics, medieval tapestries, Etruscan and Babylonian antiquities, Old Master drawings, and works by such artists as Memling, Bellini, and Fragonard. Turning to manuscripts and printed works, he acquired a Gutenberg Bible (the Morgan Library now possesses three, more than any other institution in the world), illuminated medieval books of hours, and handwritten letters of Jefferson, Washington, Napoleon, and

The Andrew Carnegie Mansion, featuring the Arthur Ross Terrace. The mansion is now the Smithsonian's Cooper-Hewitt National Design Museum.

Elizabeth I. Beginning with Thackeray, Morgan collected manuscripts of works by Dickens, Keats, Milton, and other authors of the first rank. The financier's trove of paintings, sculptures, and works on paper eventually required a home of their own, and so Morgan commissioned McKim, Mead & White to create the neoclassical library building adjacent to his brownstone home at Madison Avenue and East 36th Street in Manhattan. This building, at the heart of which is Morgan's ornate private study, is today's Morgan Library, one of New York's great museums and reference institutions. The institution's first director remarked that it "apparently contains everything but the original tablets of the Ten Commandments." She was using only mild exaggeration. Opened at the bequest of Morgan's son in 1924, 11 years after the great banker's death, it is as much a monument to its creator as that billion-dollar edifice called U.S. Steel.

ANDREW CARNEGIE

The cornerstone of Morgan's great steel trust was the colossal iron and steel business of Andrew Carnegie, the one great figure of the age of American winner-take-all capitalism who is remembered as much for his philanthropies as for the way in which he amassed his riches. To the ages, Carnegie means—Carnegie *is*—libraries, more than 2,500 of them throughout the English-speaking world, 1,689 in the United States alone. The libraries, donated to communities that agreed to provide them with land and an annual budget, were only part of his bequests, which by the time of his death in 1919 exceeded $350 million.

"Little Andy" Carnegie—he would grow to an adult height of only five feet two inches—was born in 1835 in Dumferline, Scotland, the son of a reasonably prosperous handweaver. Both his father and mother were political radicals, their beliefs a foundation for the progressive—if necessarily compromised—attitudes of the future industrialist.

With handloom weaving doomed to mechanization, the Carnegie family emigrated to western Pennsylvania in 1848. Andrew's first job was as a bobbin boy in a cotton mill, earning $1.20 a week. After that came a stint as a messenger for a telegraph company, during which he began to cultivate the contacts in the Pittsburgh business community that would serve him well in later years. Carnegie used his telegraphy skills in his next job, with the Pennsylvania Railroad, where he rose to the position of superintendent of the Pittsburgh division. He remained with the Pennsylvania until 1865, by which time his investments had become numerous and lucrative enough to enable him to strike out on his own. By far the most important of those new ventures was his controlling partnership in an iron forging company, at the threshold of an era in which iron and steel would become the physical foundation of American economic expansion.

The succession of enterprises that would by 1892 become the Carnegie Steel Company owed its phenomenal success to Andrew Carnegie's embrace of the Bessemer process after 1873, and his subsequent focus upon steel manufacture. But just as important was Carnegie's organizational genius, and his ability to delegate responsibility to talented researchers and

managers. He once suggested that his epitaph should
be, "Here lies a man who was able to surround himself
with men far cleverer than himself."

They were clever men indeed, but there is more
than a little undue self-deprecation in Carnegie's
remark. He was, after all, a man who could spot an
opportunity or a business trend with remarkable acuity,
and he was so dedicated to his work (and, it should be
said, to his widowed mother) that he didn't even marry
until he was 51 years old. But it wasn't modesty,
uncharacteristic as it was for a Gilded Age industrialist,
that startled so many of the steel man's peers. It was his
unsettling opinions on the rights of labor, extending
even to his endorsement of the idea of unions.

The man who put the phrase "Death to Privilege"
on his family's coat of arms was veering alarmingly
toward the radical politics of his ancestors—or so it
seemed to those who didn't appreciate the ambiguity of
Carnegie's professed beliefs, or the gap between what
he said and what he did. Typical was Carnegie's
dithering on such issues as the eight-hour day—first he
adopted this radical innovation, then went back to 12-
hour shifts when economy so dictated. But the worst
blight on his record was the bloody suppression of the
steel strike at a Carnegie mill in Homestead,
Pennsylvania, in 1892. Engineered not by Carnegie
himself (he was abroad at the time) but by Henry Clay
Frick, cleverest of those clever Carnegie lieutenants, the
Homestead debacle nevertheless permanently darkened
Carnegie's reputation as a friend of labor. Ultimately,
he was the responsible party.

The other great peculiarity which set Andrew
Carnegie apart from so many of his contemporaries was
his view of philanthropy. Other rich men gave away
money, but Carnegie, in his essay "The Gospel of
Wealth," was the first to articulate the idea that the
possessors of great fortunes were merely stewards,
obliged to return their riches to society.

Carnegie lived up to his own high ideals. He began
building his famous libraries in 1882, starting with a
bequest to his home town of Dumferline, Scotland.

The main staircase at Skibo Castle, the Carnegie family's retreat in Scotland. The stained glass windows show scenes from Scottish history, the farthest to the right the history of the Carnegie family.

His greatest outpouring of philanthropy, however, occurred over the nearly two decades of his life which remained after he sold his steel company to the giant U.S. Steel combine assembled by J. P. Morgan in 1901. Carnegie received nearly a half billion dollars in the sale, roughly half of which was his following payments to his associates. Carnegie was merely a conduit for this vast sum, which was soon directed not only to libraries but to the endowment of foundations that continue to underwrite research, education, and charitable projects to this day. Among them are the Carnegie Corporation of New York, endowed in 1911 with $125 million; the Carnegie Institute of Washington; the Carnegie United Kingdom Trust; and the Carnegie Trust for the Universities of Scotland. He also gave liberally to institutions promoting peace, and built the Hague Peace Palace in the Netherlands as a center for international arbitration. All in all, Carnegie managed to give away some $350 million in his lifetime, and—after reasonable provisions for his wife, daughter, and other relatives—his coffers were virtually empty when his will was probated.

By no means did Andrew Carnegie live as a pauper in order to finance his philanthropies. He was happy to spend substantial amounts on such sentimental frivolities as an 1881 coach trip throughout the length of Great Britain, crowned by his triumphal entry into Dumferline to make his library donation in person. In 1897, he bought the ruined castle of Skibo in the Scottish Highlands, and spent lavishly to transform it into a romantic ideal of a laird's estate complete with salmon streams, bagpipers to welcome visitors, and a vast pipe organ for entertainment at meals.

Carnegie and his family spent five months a year at Skibo; the rest of the time, they lived at the "most modest, plain, and roomiest" house he built in 1902 at Fifth Avenue and East 91st Street in Manhattan. Now the Smithsonian Institution's Cooper-Hewitt National Design Museum, the 64-room Georgian mansion *was* plain in its way, compared to the midtown palaces of other moguls, and stood in what was then a very unfashionable neighborhood—before Carnegie came along, it had been left to squatters and their shanties. Ever the practical man, Carnegie built the first private home in New York to have a steel frame, an Otis passenger elevator, and central heating. There was even a system for drawing air over tanks of cool water, in an early attempt at air conditioning.

That sense of practicality, of the virtue of a plainness that was so hard for a fabulously rich man to achieve, was a thread that ran through Andrew Carnegie's life. His library at Skibo was a telling bit of evidence: having had his friend Lord Acton recommend some eight thousand titles, he assigned the acquisition of the works to Hew Morrison, head librarian at the Carnegie Library in Edinburgh. When the books were delivered, Carnegie was deeply displeased. Without his permission, Morrison had them handsomely rebound. "I never said one word to you about changing the bindings of these gems," Carnegie wrote Morrison. The rebindings were, he went on, "an insult to the great Teachers from whom I draw my intellectual & emotional life."

HENRY CLAY FRICK

If Andrew Carnegie is remembered—to some, perhaps too charitably—as a rosy-cheeked and benign presence who scattered libraries across the land the way Johnny Appleseed did Pippins and Macs, his one-time colleague and eventual enemy Henry Clay Frick left behind a quite different set of impressions.

Unlike Carnegie, Frick was born into money; his grandfather was a wealthy distiller. Frick made his own fortune by providing coke (coal baked to eliminate impurities and leave pure carbon) to the burgeoning western Pennsylvania iron and steel industries, eventually integrating his business with that of Carnegie and becoming chairman of the Scotsman's vast enterprise.

Frick, as we saw earlier, was under no illusions as to the rights of labor. "Of all slave drivers, for spite and kick,/ No one so cruel as Tyrant Frick," went the chorus of a poem that appeared in a union publication during the steel man's heyday. If it can be argued that the American business landscape was heavily populated with slave drivers at the time, there is no denying that Frick's devotion to opposing organized labor and employing scab workers was particularly ardent. He was one of the few Gilded Age captains of industry to actually have been the target of an assassination attempt: in the aftermath of the Homestead debacle, Frick was shot and seriously wounded by a young anarchist named Alexander Berkman, who had presented himself at the executive's office. This incident, and the fact that Carnegie eventually muscled

Frick out of his company ("I'll see him in hell, where we
both are going," was Frick's reply to a proposed
reconciliation shortly before his death in 1919), would
rank among the salient events of Frick's life—if it
weren't for the man's outstanding achievements as an
art collector and museum benefactor.

Frick began collecting paintings seriously around
1895, his tastes at first running to the French Barbizon
School but eventually deepening to include Flemish,
Dutch, Italian, and Spanish masters. In 1906, he
bought an entire Manhattan block, on Fifth Avenue
between 70th and 71st streets, and commissioned
Carrere & Hastings, architects of the New York Public
Library, to build a $4 million neoclassical mansion on
the site. Finished in 1914, it was meant to serve both as
a home for the Frick family and, eventually, as an art
museum. (Ironically, one of the reasons Frick left his
turreted Pittsburgh mansion was that he felt the steel
city's air was bad for his paintings.)

After the death of Frick's widow in 1931, the white
stone pile on Fifth Avenue was subtly transformed from
a cool, formal home into an intimate and engaging
gallery. Splendid works by Tiepolo and Fragonard,
Van Eyck and Vermeer, Holbein and Watteau are
among the treasures of the Frick Collection, things of
great beauty enshrined in the personal palace of a man
who was all coke and iron.

JOHN DAVISON ROCKEFELLER

When J. P. Morgan died, and his taxable estate was
tallied at $77.5 million, one of his contemporaries archly
remarked, "And to think that he wasn't even a rich

man." There was only a handful of individuals on earth who could have spoken those words with anything like a straight face; and in fact they were spoken by the man with the straightest face of all. The son of a rascally traveling salesman whom Morgan's family would have cut dead socially, he had successfully come to grips with America's newfound appetite for petroleum. His name was John Davison Rockefeller.

Although at least one modern mogul's paper fortune is 50 times as large as Rockefeller's in 2002 dollars, no American was ever richer in terms of the percentage of the gross domestic product his holdings represented. At his peak, Rockefeller was worth just shy of one billion dollars. In 1902, he earned the equivalent of a modern billion—$58 million—in dividends from his Standard Oil Corporation and other investments. His sister said it best: "When it was raining porridge, John's dish was always right side up."

John's dish, and the porridge that filled it, have long been the stuff of American legend. There used to be a line in a 1950s commercial jingle, "Better coffee Rockefeller's money can't buy," and although the Rockefeller family asked the coffee company to change the wording to "a millionaire's money," it's a telling fact that years after the departure of John D. Senior, his name and that of his descendants remained a synonym for fathomless wealth.

To the extent that we still retain an image of Rockefeller the man, 65 years after his death, it is an image of a frail, parchment-skinned character with birdlike features and a prim, almost otherworldy expression: a hairless alien from the planet Money. If

that is the lasting impression, it is because Rockefeller lasted so long. He died in 1937, just short of his 98th birthday, and for the last 40 years of his life he was the victim of alopecia, a disease which causes the loss of body hair. By 1901, his body was as smooth as an egg. He couldn't do much about eyebrows, but he kept a collection of wigs in varying lengths, and wore them in succession to look as if he were going from one haircut to another.

The Rockefeller of the 19th century was a different creature altogether, a trim, straight-backed man with a dark moustache who allowed himself neither the paunch nor the extravagant whiskers of other magnificoes of his age. He was a product of the nondescript villages of upstate New York—was there ever a more fertile breeding ground for future tycoons?—and he came of age in the new midwest metropolis of Cleveland, Ohio, where his father had brought the family in the early 1850s. It was there that Rockefeller got his first job, as an assistant bookkeeper in a produce and commodities shipping firm. Cleveland was also the young man's playing field when, at the age of 18, he launched a partnership as a commission merchant.

Because of Cleveland's proximity to the newly discovered oilfields of western Pennsylvania, petroleum soon became one of the commodities in which Rockefeller traded. When the opportunity arose, he moved into refining. Those were the years when kerosene was taking over from whale oil as America's principal source of illumination, and Rockefeller's fortune was secured by the thirst of millions of lamps long before Henry Ford created a demand for another petroleum distillate, gasoline, which of course Rockefeller's Standard Oil Company was ready and eager to supply.

Rockefeller's meteoric rise from Cleveland refiner of kerosene to master of the greatest of all preregulation American monopolies was the result not only of spiraling demand, but of the industrialist's now-legendary demolishing of competition by, among other means, forcing railroads to give his high-volume business preferential shipping rates. The black side of the Rockefeller legend grew accordingly, so that by the time of the court-ordered breakup of Standard Oil into several regional companies (a process that only made Rockefeller richer, since he owned stock in all of them), he was excoriated by the muckraking press as a gouging manipulator, the man who had finally taken capitalism too far. But there was always another side to John D. Rockefeller, and the decades of his long retirement gave him ample occasion to show it. He was, quite simply, the greatest of all American philanthropists.

Even as a young bookkeeper making only several hundred dollars a year, Rockefeller earmarked a portion of his wages for charitable contributions. If his strict Baptist faith gave him the assurance that a man ought to work hard and earn all he could, it also imbued him with the notion that the money was to be reinvested in the community through philanthropy. During his lifetime he gave away $530 million, primarily to educational and research institutions—"Instead of giving alms to beggars," he once remarked, "[it is more worthwhile] to remove the causes which lead to the existence of beggars." He also handed out his famous dimes, thousands of them, not as alms but as tokens representing thrift. The dimes also provided an outlet for the puckish side of John D.'s nature. Despite the common impression of him as a grim old moneybags, he had a considerable dry wit.

Rockefeller the devout, Sunday-School teacher Baptist also avoided the extravagance and show of his plutocrat peers. He smoked no cigars, rented no

private rooms at Delmonico's for champagne-soaked soirees, captained no yachts, and kept no bejeweled mistresses. Certainly he was no miser of the Hetty Green stamp—that Wall Street operator was worth tens of millions, yet she lived in a walkup flat in Hoboken. Rockefeller dressed soberly but well, and kept a huge, rambling summer home outside Cleveland even after he moved to a New York brownstone. Perhaps his greatest extravagance was his estate at Pocantico Hills, in New York's Westchester County, but the building of Kykuit, his mansion on the property, originated with his son, John D. Rockefeller, Jr.

The younger Rockefeller hired architects Chester Aldrich and William Delano to create a 1906 house with a wraparound porch and steep-sloped roof and dormers, barely more than upper-middle class in its outward appearance. But between 1911 and 1913, Junior had the facade transformed into the classically pilastered and pedimented version that exists today, with a full third floor replacing those bourgeois dormers. And yet the house remained a modest mansion rather than a billionaire's palace, in keeping with Rockefeller Senior's simple tastes. Its most majestic aspect is its view of the Hudson River valley, and its greatest extravagance was the old man's private golf course. His religion forbade him cards and dancing, but golf was good exercise in God's fresh air.

RETAIL MAGNATES

Toward the close of the 19th century, great new fortunes again owed their existence to the business of selling things. But these were different times than those

"I am more drawn to the plastic, three-dimensional, than to pure line and color," said Nelson Rockefeller; Henry Moore was a favorite sculptor.

in which the Derbys and Crowninshields of Salem made their money by importing luxury goods and leaving them for others to merchandise. The mercantile Midases of the late Victorian age were shopkeepers on a grand scale, men who built multistory temples of commerce. Or, in the case of individuals like Aaron Montgomery Ward and Richard Warren Sears (the man who hired Alvah C. Roebuck to repair his mail-order watches), they created their empires out of catalogues rather than bricks and mortar.

Back in the days when Commodore Vanderbilt was piling up his steamship dollars, an Irish immigrant and one-time schoolteacher named Alexander Turney Stewart was building America's first retail fortune. Beginning in 1823, and eventually operating out of a six-story "marble palace" (it was actually painted cast iron) on lower Broadway, A. T. Stewart ran a dry goods business that catered to the New York carriage trade, carrying the finest in silks, lace, cashmere, and ready-made Paris gowns. Stewart employed some two hundred clerks, whom he personally instructed in package wrapping techniques that would save paper and string, and took in $3 million a year during the mid-1800s.

Moody and unpleasant in disposition, allegedly quite stingy with his employees, Stewart was largely ostracized from Knickerbocker society. But if he sulked over his exclusion from the company of the people who wore the finery he imported, at least he was able to do so in what was in its time the largest mansion in New York—a pillared palazzo on Fifth Avenue at 34th Street built, unlike his store, out of real marble. By the end of

Stewart's life, he was one of the three richest men in New York. The others were Cornelius Vanderbilt and William Backhouse Astor, John Jacob Astor's son.

Stewart's establishment was, strictly speaking, an enormous dry goods store, and not a department store in the modern sense. But his innovation of assigning plainly displayed, no-haggle prices on his merchandise was adopted by later retailers whose fame and fortunes rested on huge, multi-department operations that quickly became the model for emporiums throughout the United States. Rowland Hussey Macy, a

Nantucketer who served for four years on a whaling ship while still in his teens and later tried his hand at selling provisions to miners during the California gold rush, took up the fixed-price policy when he and his brother opened a dry goods store in Haverhill, Massachusetts, in 1851. The Haverhill venture failed, but Macy at age 36 was ready to give retailing one more try. He opened his new business as R. H. Macy and Company, on 14th Street in Manhattan, on October 28, 1858.

The stocky, full-bearded R. H. Macy drove himself

hard, determined to find in middle age the success that had eluded him for years. He had a sharp temper and a sailor's command of profanity, and some of his attempts at keeping overhead down were almost comical. He wouldn't hear of having shades on his gas lamps, saying that since he had paid for the gas, he wanted the light unimpeded. But several of his innovations have a decidedly modern ring: Macy's, in its founder's day, pioneered the idea of using prices such as "$4.99" to make an item look cheaper than one marked at $5.00, and by 1875—two years before R. H. Macy's death—the store's advertisements declared, "We will not be undersold." As for other Macy's traditions, history has not told us what R. H. thought of Thanksgiving Day parades.

Marshall Field, born in Massachusetts' Berkshire Hills in 1834, struck out for Chicago at the age of 22. He was so intent on setting aside capital that when he was hired as a clerk in a wholesale dry goods firm, he lived in the store in order to save half of his $400 annual salary. Eight years later, having become a partner and general manager, his interest in the business was worth $260,000. By 1881, the firm whose back room he had once slept in was known as Marshall Field & Company. Quiet and unassuming, Field kept a low profile in Chicago social circles but was everywhere at once in his store. He pioneered the use of advertising to create a demand for goods he had already purchased, rather than wait for demand—and wholesale prices—to rise on their own.

Marshall Field donated the land for the new University of Chicago, and his bequests made possible the city's Field Museum of Natural History. The retailer surely had a sentimental streak, because the gift he was proudest of was that of a library to his hometown of Conway, Massachusetts. Another, less tangible part of his legacy lives on wherever retailers remember who they are working for: coming upon one of his clerks arguing with a customer one day, Field spoke the words that became his store's motto: "Give the lady what she wants."

With the population of the United States expanding rapidly during the last decades of the 19th century, the carriage trade wasn't the only path to retail riches. One man who realized this was Frank Winfield Woolworth, who managed to pay cash to build the tallest building in the world—cash, his contemporaries enjoyed remarking, that had come to him in the form of five- and ten-cent pieces.

Unlike R. H. Macy, who drifted into retailing, F. W. Woolworth seems to have had his heart set on selling things right from the start. Born on a northern New York State farm in 1854, he took a job at age 19 as a general store clerk just for the experience, drawing no wages for the first three months. In 1878, he talked his employer into trying a new gimmick he had heard about, a table stocked with goods priced at a uniform five cents.

Staked by his former boss, F. W. Woolworth opened his first store in Utica, New York, in 1879. Every item sold for a nickel—but those nickels added up to only $150 in profits after three months, so Woolworth closed the doors of his shabby rented premises and went off to try again in Lancaster, Pennsylvania. This time, things sold so well that the young man expanded to a couple of other Pennsylvania cities, hired his brother to help him, and took a chance on a table of ten-cent items at his new Scranton location. It was there that the famous sign first went up: "5 & 10 cent store."

By the early 1890s, there were some thirty Woolworth stores, and sales had surpassed $1 million a year. The 20-year path from that landmark to another—the Woolworth Building, the 720-foot Gothic-inspired "Cathedral of Commerce" completed in 1913—was a steady story of Woolworth store openings on both sides of the Atlantic, and of the founder's transformation from a lean, hungry young man to a 250-pound, white-mustached tycoon whose doctors were perpetually warning him that he was digging his grave with a fork. F. W. Woolworth, who largely ignored the physicians (he died just shy of his 65th birthday in 1919), was a man whose tastes in his maturity extended not only to gargantuan meals and posh suites on ocean liners, and to the usual architectural excesses of his peers, but to music—specifically, organ music.

Woolworth loved to show off the great pipe organ he had installed in the drawing room of his Fifth Avenue mansion. He had a hand in designing it himself, creating an instrument that operated like an enormous player piano with controls that would not only synchronize the music with displays of colored lights, but with illuminated paintings of the composers whose works were being played. As his father put it during a visit to the house, "Well, Frank, you always did like to lay it on thick." And as the old man

bemusedly admired his son's musical extravagance, no doubt the piano tinkled in yet another new Woolworth's store, as a clerk sat at the keyboard to promote the latest sheet-music tune. That emporium, in the eyes of its distant owner, was an undoubted boon to its community. "The more stores we create," F. W. Woolworth once said, "the more good we do for humanity."

JOSEPH PULITZER

If selling was a path to riches as the 20th century approached, so was telling. The idea of a press empire was something new in the world, a phenomenon made possible by the twin advances of wider literacy and mechanized printing. As Joseph Pulitzer cruised in his yacht between Jeykll Island, Georgia, and Bar Harbor, Maine, or surveyed Manhattan from his office perch in the dome of the *World* Building on Park Row, he may not have mused on how much he owed to the success of public education, or to the development of the rotary press earlier in the 1800s; but those developments had nonetheless put him where he was. And that was at the pinnacle of the American newspaper industry.

Joseph Pulitzer was a man of paradoxes. Brought up comfortably in Hungary, where he was born in 1847, he had to struggle as a young man in the United States after his family lost its money. He launched his career writing for German-language newspapers, but began his meteoric rise after purchasing the English-language St. Louis *Evening Dispatch* and creating that city's *Post-Dispatch* in 1878. His greatest achievement was the transformation of the New York *World*, nearly

moribund when he bought it from Jay Gould in 1883, into a great liberal organ—and yet in his personal life, Pulitzer surrounded himself with much the same luxury as the captains of industry whose power and excesses he excoriated.

Pulitzer was a great shaper of public opinion, yet he chose to remain aloof from the back-room politics that attract many powerful publishers. "He believed in Liberty, Equality, and Opportunity," his biographer Don Seitz wrote. "Fraternity was not in his code." The aloof press czar put a tangible stamp on his hatred of intrusion, creating soundproof rooms at his homes in New York and Bar Harbor. He worked himself into infirmity and blindness, but was so fond of music as a means of relaxation that he always included a competent pianist among his secretaries.

Perhaps most paradoxical of all is the fact that the immensely cultured Pulitzer, whose great legacy is the series of prizes honoring literary, journalistic, and musical excellence, was the man most responsible for nurturing the strain of sensationalism in the American press. Or perhaps not: receiving guests at his home, his favorite greeting was, "Tell me a good story." Whether Pulitzer Prize material or red meat from the police blotter, "a good story" was at the heart of this master pressman's business.

In 1883, the year Joseph Pulitzer bought the New York *World*, a rich young man from California was managing a successful circulation drive for the Harvard University humor magazine, the *Lampoon*. Within three years he had dropped out of Harvard—he always had a problem with authority, and was an indifferent student at best—and gone to New York to take a reporter's job on the *World*. All the while, he was pestering his father to give him a money-losing paper, the San Francisco *Examiner*, which the older man owned. Father finally capitulated, and William Randolph Hearst never looked back.

Titans of the Early Twentieth Century

ILLIAM Randolph Hearst is the only great American tycoon known as much through a fictional portrayal as through his actual persona. Ever since Orson Welles gave us the figure of Charles Foster Kane in his 1941 film *Citizen Kane*, art has blurred reality in our understanding of the Hearst saga. But the real William Randolph Hearst was a character who lived, worked, and played on an even larger scale than Welles's creation.

Hearst began his rise in the newspaper industry on the strength of his father's success in an entirely different pursuit. George Hearst was one of the men made into millionaires by Nevada's Comstock Lode of silver ore; in later life, he became a California land baron and a member of the state's U.S. Senate delegation. His foray into newspaper ownership with the *Examiner* was merely a political maneuver. For William Randolph Hearst, who talked his father into letting him take over the paper in 1887, the transformation of the *Examiner* was an object in itself.

Hearst turned the *Examiner* around, employing a mix of banner headlines, sensationalized writing, and campaigns for civic reform. Moving into his old training ground—and the domain of Joseph Pulitzer—he bought the New York *Morning Journal* in 1895 and applied the same methods, hiring top editorial talent away from Pulitzer and pioneering the use of Sunday comics and "sob sister" columns. The *Journal* was the primary vehicle for Hearst's first, and still most notorious, nationwide campaign: the stirring of war fever over Spanish colonial occupation of Cuba. The publisher backed Cuban insurgency against Spain, and instructed his correspondents to exaggerate (and in some instances manufacture) instances of Spanish atrocity in putting down the rebellion. "You furnish the pictures and I'll furnish the war," was his legendary reply to artist Frederic Remington, issued after Remington reported that there was "no

(ABOVE)
An aerial view of La Cuesta Encantada, "the Enchanted Hill."

(OPPOSITE)
Working with architect Julia Morgan, William Randolph Hearst began work on La Casa Grande, crown jewel of his San Simeon estate, in 1919.

(FOLLOWING SPREAD)
Hearst told Julia Morgan that he wanted to build "a little something": La Cuesta Encantada rises above the coastal mist.

"Castle in the Clouds"
In 1919 William Randolph Hearst gave sim-
ple instructions to San Francisco architect
Julia Morgan: "...we are tired of camping out
in the open at the ranch in San Simeon and I
would like to build a little something." That
little something developed into "La Cuesta
Encantada"—The Enchanted Hill. Hearst
and Julia Morgan collaborated for 28 years
to construct Hearst's lifetime dream and one
of the world's greatest showplaces.
Photo: Victoria Garagliano. © Hearst Castle®/CA State
Parks.

trouble" in Cuba. Of course Hearst got his war, following the sinking of the USS *Maine* in Havana harbor. Hearst's papers trumpeted Spain's responsibility for the tragedy, even though it still remains a mystery nearly a century later.

Flush with the success his sensationalized Spanish-American War reportage had brought to his papers, Hearst rapidly expanded his press holdings during the early decades of the 20th century. He added Chicago papers in 1900 and 1902, and entered the Boston and Los Angeles markets in 1904. By 1927 Hearst was publishing 25 dailies and 17 Sunday papers in 17 cities. Twenty-four magazines were eventually added to the Hearst fold, as were radio stations, newsreels, and motion-picture production. It has been estimated that by the late 1940s, one-third of the U.S. population—some 40 million people—were readers of Hearst publications. And they heard directly from the man at the center of this empire: Hearst was constantly on the phone with his underlings, directing editorial policy, and was himself the author of columns and editorials published throughout his newspaper chain.

Sensationalism was Hearst's constant modus operandi, but the causes it served shifted over the course of his long career. Originally enough of a reformer to have supported the 1896 and 1900 presidential candidacies of populist William Jennings Bryan and fumed against the Standard Oil monopoly, Hearst grew increasingly conservative; his early support of Franklin Roosevelt evaporated during FDR's first term, and a Hearst visit with Adolf Hitler in 1934 left the publisher open to charges that he was a

The indoor Roman Pool at La Casa Grande was inspired by an ancient Roman bath.

fascist sympathizer. Throughout the first three decades of his career Hearst pursued his own political ambitions, succeeding in getting elected to the U.S. House of Representatives but failing in bids for the Senate, New York City mayoralty, and New York State governorship. Like Charles Foster Kane in *Citizen Kane,* his great goal was the presidency. But he came no closer than a vigorous battle for the Democratic nomination in 1904.

William Randolph Hearst's thwarted political longings pale before his success as creator of the grandest personal surroundings ever enjoyed by an American plutocrat. He was an inveterate and omnivorous collector, spending an estimated million dollars a year on art and antiques. Hearst enjoyed the luxury of distributing his acquisitions among a string of lavish estates, including his home in New York, his Welsh castle, and his Bavarian-style retreat near Mt. Shasta. But the greatest architectural obsession of the publisher's life—and, at perhaps $30 million, the most expensive residence ever constructed by an American— was the California estate today known as "Hearst Castle," which its builder called "La Cuesta Encantada"—the Enchanted Hill.

The palette on which Hearst worked was the Piedra Blanca Ranch, a 48,000-acre property near San Simeon that his father had bought in 1865. Hiring Julia Morgan, America's first notable woman architect, he began to piece together his dream castle in 1919, when he was already 56 years old. Hearst would build at San Simeon for most of the rest of his life, all the while using the place to entertain luminaries ranging from Buster

(ABOVE)

Whimsical characters adorn the wrought-iron doors made by Edward Trinkkeller, a California craftsman, at la Casa Grande.

(RIGHT)

The Refectory at la Casa Grande: Hearst made sure there was a bottle of ketchup within reach of each of his dinner guests.

Keaton to Winston Churchill. It was also the ultimate stage setting for his mistress, Marion Davies, a Hollywood actress whose career he relentlessly promoted and whose relationship with him he made no effort to conceal—even as Hearst papers stood as champions of what a later generation would call "family values."

The twin Mediterranean towers of the main house, La Casa Grande, stand 137 feet high, and the scale of everything else on the Enchanted Hill is cued to their grand proportions . . . and to the grand proportions of Hearst himself, all six feet three inches and 220 pounds of him. There are 56 bedrooms, 61 bathrooms, 41 fireplaces, and terraces designers were told to treat as "rooms without walls." At the center of it all was a refectory with a dining table that could seat 22 guests, none of whom had to reach far for the bottles of ketchup that Hearst insisted accompany every dinner. It was a nice proletarian touch, for a man who had bought the contents of European palaces and monasteries—entire rooms, stained glass windows, elaborately carved staircases and paneling, tapestries—and installed them in his castle as patents of the New World nobility he craved for himself.

Hearst's landscaping at San Simeon—now a California state historic site—rivals La Casa Grande and its surrounding pools, terraces, and guest houses. He thought nothing of having mature oak and cypress trees moved and replanted, or of planting a barren hilltop with pines even though a road had to be built for the purpose. He kept a private zoo, and played night tennis on a court lit by 28 1000-watt bulbs.

One guest, George Bernard Shaw, is said to have remarked of San Simeon, "It's the way God would have done it, if He had Hearst's money." Ultimately, even Hearst didn't have the money. The place was still unfinished when he died, at age 88, in 1951.

Men such as Joseph Pulitzer, William Randolph Hearst, and, later, the Time-Life titan Henry Luce took journalism out of an era in which it had been a local product meant primarily for local consumption, and made it into a vehicle for mass culture in what Luce would herald as the "American Century." During the decade of Hearst's first great triumphs, the 1890s, a power-station engineer from Dearborn, Michigan, would create an actual rather than a figurative vehicle, one easily recognizable in the advertising pages of Hearst and Luce publications for years to come. Mass-produced popular culture was one of two great hallmarks of the American Century, and the mass-produced automobile was the other. It was created by Henry Ford.

HENRY FORD

With the exception of John D. Rockefeller, Sr., no American capitalist has so captured the world's imagination as Henry Ford. In Aldous Huxley's novel *Brave New World*, the phrase "the year of Our Ford" is substituted for "A.D." to indicate the debt owed the industrialist by an advanced technological society. The facts of Ford's life are legend: He built his first car, the "Quadricycle," in 1896, and was able to drive it on the streets of Dearborn only after taking a sledge-hammer to the doorway of the shed he used as a

(ABOVE)

Henry Ford enjoys his son Edsel's performance at the player piano during a camping trip in Maryland, 1921.

(RIGHT)

Henry and Clara Ford at Fair Lane, with grandchildren Henry II and — in Henry's lap — Benson Ford, 1923.

(ABOVE)

Henry Ford demonstrates a prototype at his Detroit plant, 1907. A year later, he sold the first of 15 million Model Ts.

PHOTO FROM THE COLLECTIONS OF HENRY FORD MUSEUM & GREENFIELD VILLAGE.

(RIGHT)

Henry Ford (far right) on a 1920s fishing trip with Thomas Edison (next to Ford) and Harvey Firestone (second from left). At far left is Christian Edison, the inventor's son.

PHOTO LIBRARY OF CONGRESS.

(ABOVE)

Henry and Clara Ford, on a 1906 trip to the Grand Canyon. The automaker had a lifelong love of the outdoors.

PHOTO FROM THE COLLECTIONS OF HENRY FORD MUSEUM & GREENFIELD VILLAGE.

(LEFT)

The Fords visit England during the late 1920s: at right are Lady Nancy Astor and her son, William Waldorf Astor.

PHOTO LIBRARY OF CONGRESS.

workshop. After several false starts manufacturing more expensive cars, he introduced the inexpensive, mass-produced Model T in 1908 and captured nearly one-half of the world automobile market within 10 years. Along the Rouge River near Detroit, he built the first completely vertically integrated automobile plant, capable of taking iron ore and coke and turning them into cars—and then, in a move that the *Wall Street Journal* called "the most foolish thing ever attempted in the industrial world," he saw to it that his workers could afford the machines they were building by paying

them an unheard-of five dollars a day.

Henry Ford, a lean, plainspoken Midwesterner raised on a farm and a stranger to wealth and fame until he was in his forties, had one of the most complex and contradictory natures of all the great American captains of industry. The man who could bestow five dollars a day on his employees was also capable of creating a "sociological department" that would visit workers' homes to make sure they and their families were living in a seemly manner and not squandering the Ford largesse—and, much

The Field Room, with its massive stone fireplace
from a nearby tavern, was a favorite evening
gathering place for Ford family and friends.

PHOTO FAIR LANE (THE HENRY AND CLARA BRYANT FORD HOUSE).

worse, allow his henchman Harry Bennett to use his company security apparatus to viciously put down attempts at unionization during the 1930s. (In 1932, four pro-union marchers were shot dead by Dearborn police working closely with Ford security.)

The very model of the practical engineer, as comfortable in the machine shop as behind his desk, Henry Ford could nevertheless extol the transcendental philosophy of Ralph Waldo Emerson, and became a believer in reincarnation. Responsible for accelerating the pace of American urbanization and transforming rural landscapes across the continent, he remained all his life a lover of nature, particularly birds, and struck up a friendship with the great naturalist John Burroughs, with whom he went on several camping trips. (Thomas Edison joined these excursions, as did tire manufacturer Harvey Firestone.) And at Dearborn, Ford created Greenfield Village, a vast assemblage of museum-piece historic structures honoring small-town pre-industrial America, even as his automobiles helped the nation put an incalculable distance between its past and its future.

Ford was an idealist and pacifist who sought to end World War I by traveling to Europe in 1915 on a "Peace Ship," remarking that he wanted "to make the world a little better for having lived in it." He was an early champion of fair wages and employment practices for blacks, who made up 10 percent of his workforce by 1926 and could even be promoted to supervisory positions over whites. Yet in his newspaper venture of the early 1920s, the *Dearborn Independent*, he published a continuous stream of anti-Semitic invective apparently born of his identification of Jews with an international banking conspiracy.

By 1918, virtually half of all the automobiles on earth were Model Ts, and the success of his plain, reliable little car ("any color you like, as long as it's black") had brought Ford's wealth near the billion-dollar mark. He was not the man to spend it lavishly; sometimes, as in the case of the uncashed $75,000 check his wife once found in one of his suit pockets, he didn't spend it at all—but he did build an estate. With a characteristic nod to nostalgia, he named it Fair Lane, after the district in the Irish city of Cork where his grandfather had once lived. Also characteristic was Ford's siting of his mansion not in the fashionable Detroit suburb of Grosse Point, but in his boyhood home of Dearborn, where one day he would also construct Greenfield Village.

Ford spent a million 1914 dollars to build Fair Lane, and it is pleasant to imagine what that sum could have bought if it had been placed in the hands of Frank Lloyd Wright, the carmaker's original choice as architect. Wright was unavailable, though, and the task devolved to a pair of lesser talents who came up with a dull limestone fortress that hardly did more for its Rouge River setting than the Ford factory downstream.

Its stodgy appearance aside, Fair Lane did have its comforts. Bathroom faucets offered either well or rainwater, hot and cold, as well as hot-air jets for hair drying. There was an indoor swimming pool, a bowling alley, and a golf course. Ford could relax in a rustic den whose fireplace mantel bore Thoreau's admonition, "Chop your own wood, and it will warm you twice."

The bulk of the mansion's energy supply, however, was dependent on a powerhouse that Ford had designed himself. Its generators ran on water power from a dam in the Rouge River, and polished brass instruments shone against its green walls with marble trimming. Best of all, for the man who counted John Burroughs among his friends, was the maze of heating pipes that extended outdoors to keep five hundred birdbaths from freezing in winter.

Born during the Civil War, in an America vastly different from the one he and his machines helped create, Henry Ford died at 83 in 1947. That would be the Year of Our Ford 39, if we mark the beginning of the era with the introduction of the Model T.

Henry Ford's heyday coincided with the years in which dozens of entrepreneurs put their names on hubcaps and radiators. Many of those names have long survived the shakeout of independent auto companies that reached its peak in the 1920s and '30s and still continues today; many others did not. Buick, Dodge, Olds, Nash, Willys, Packard: these were all men, not merely cars. One such name survives not only on an automobile, but in the most beautiful Art Deco building in the world.

WALTER P. CHRYSLER

Walter P. Chrysler was the Kansas-born son of a Union Pacific engineer. He trained as a machinist in railroad maintenance shops, eventually becoming superintendent of a locomotive plant. But his life truly began on a day in 1908 when he fell in love with a gleaming new Locomobile at an auto show in Chicago. Chrysler borrowed most of the $5,000 needed to buy the Locomobile, which he took apart and put back together repeatedly until he understood its every working. His first professional involvement with cars came in 1911, when he went to work for the Buick Motor Company; 14 years later, having risen to a vice-presidency at the new General Motors and retired a millionaire, he created the Chrysler Corporation at the age of 50. The remaining 15 years of his life secured his reputation as an automotive visionary, a master machinist-manager. They also gave him the opportunity to place his name on

(ABOVE)
His company's name has been diluted by merger, but Walter Chrysler will always be associated with New York's most sublime skyscraper.
PHOTO LIBRARY OF CONGRESS.

(OPPOSITE TOP)
Mr. and Mrs. Walter Chrysler, with another Chrysler in the background, Palm Beach, 1937.
PHOTO MORGAN COLLECTION/GETTY IMAGES.

(OPPOSITE BOTTOM)
Art collector Walter Chrysler, Jr., son of the automaker, at a 1950 sale of his Impressionist paintings.
PHOTO GETTY IMAGES.

a sublime inanimate object that shouted out its connection with the motor age.

The Chrysler Corporation didn't build the Chrysler Building; Walter Chrysler did. Designed by William Van Alen and completed at a cost of $14 million in 1930, the sleek structure was topped with a crested, elongated dome and spire of chromium nickel steel and ornamented with enormous replicas of Chrysler hubcaps and radiator caps. It reigned as the tallest structure in the world until the Empire State Building was completed in 1931. When we look at the untarnished majesty of that Art Deco dome today, it's hard to imagine it as anything other than a public monument. When the Chrysler Building was new, though, it reportedly had one very special private aspect. Two flights up from Walter Chrysler's baronial 56th-floor office, contemporary sources reported, was a duplex apartment designed for Chrysler himself. No photographs of this aerie exist—but breakfast at Tiffany's aside, it is hard to imagine a more spectacular New York experience than living in the Chrysler Building. And it was a midwestern machinist who did.

One of the most respected American entrepreneurs of the 20th century was a notable failure as an automaker. Only those who are well into their fifties, or who are dedicated auto buffs, remember cars called the Kaiser, the Frazer, or the Henry J. Manufactured during the late 1940s and early '50s, they were the creations of Henry J. Kaiser and his partner, Joseph Frazer; the Henry J. was a stripped-down economy car (one early suggestion for its name, ironically enough, had been "Mustang") that appeared at the beginning of a decade that would be known for chrome ostentation. But Henry J. Kaiser was too much of a success at virtually everything else he attempted to be remembered for a failed carmaking enterprise.

Born in 1882 in upstate New York—again, was there something in the water?—Kaiser first tasted success as a paving contractor on both sides of the U.S.–Canadian border in the Pacific Northwest. (His future father-in-law had told Kaiser he would deny him his daughter's hand in marriage unless he sold his interest in a Lake Placid photography shop and started earning real money.) The contractor's big break came in 1931, when a consortium his company had joined won the bid to build Hoover Dam, on the Colorado River in Nevada. Attacking the job with an energy remarkable in a fat, placid-looking man, Kaiser finished the job on time and later went on to build the Grand Coulee Dam on Washington's Columbia River.

Kaiser's greatest achievement, though, came when he entered the shipbuilding industry at the outset of World War II. With Navy contracts in hand, this supremely capable marshaler of men and materials turned out 1,490 vessels between 1941 and 1945, including 821 of the 10,000-ton "Liberty Ships" that lumbered through the world's oceans carrying supplies for the Allied effort. Using the subassembly method, in which major portions of each ship were prefabricated then brought together only as needed, Kaiser's workers trimmed months from traditional production schedules. One crew actually managed to assemble a Liberty Ship in four days, 15 hours, and 26 minutes from the time the keel was laid.

Kaiser's name echoed down through the postwar years in the steel and aluminum industries, in television broadcasting, and of course in the money-losing Kaiser-Frazer enterprise. It survives to this day in the Kaiser-Permanente health maintenance organization, an outgrowth of a medical plan he created for his workers. But Kaiser's reputation as a paragon of the can-do spirit was secured during those frantic days of World War II, when Liberty ships came down the ways like rolls from an oven.

GEORGE EASTMAN

On broad, handsome East Avenue in Rochester, New York, stands a stately Georgian Revival mansion that houses one of the world's greatest museums of photography. Its spacious rooms contain not only the museum collections, but also many reminders that the man who built the place was very up-to-date: how many houses had central vacuum systems in 1905? If kitchen aromas lingered over the decades, though, they would convey something a good deal more quirky. George Eastman, who brought photography to the masses,

liked to relax not in a darkroom but by baking lemon pies.

If lemon pies seem a modest amusement for a man once estimated to be the sixth richest in the nation, remember that George Eastman was himself so unassuming that a newly hired watchman at his factory once turned him away at the gate when he stated his name, replying, "Glad to meet you, I'm John D. Rockefeller." Perhaps the watchman had never seen Eastman's photograph—an irony in itself—or perhaps, he had, and simply couldn't associate that kindly, serious, high-school-principal face with the name on his paycheck. That name was ubiquitous in Rochester, but the face was seldom in the society pages.

Thanks to George Eastman, photography itself was ubiquitous by the beginning of the 20th century. As a 23-year-old bank employee in 1877, Eastman had spent nearly 50 dollars on a camera. In the Rochester of that day, there were only two other amateur photographers—the wet plate process was that complicated. Eastman mastered it, and indeed became so enamored of photography that he did little else with his spare time. But he felt the whole procedure could be simplified. With his 1878 invention of a machine that would coat photographic plates with an emulsion of gelatin and silver bromide, followed by his development of paper-backed roll film several years later, Eastman had done just that. In 1888, he put his roll film into a hand-held camera he called the "Kodak," having coined the name because he liked the "firm and unyielding" sound of the letter "k."

The George Eastman who moved into his newly

finished mansion in 1905 had made a resounding success of his Eastman Kodak Company, but he never stopped improving his products. His was the genius behind the development of motion-picture film for the Edison-invented cameras that made possible a great new medium for entertainment and information; in the 1920s, he would even accompany the explorers Osa and Martin Johnson as they took Eastman films on safari to record a rapidly vanishing Africa. He ran a huge business, far and away the leader in the industry it had pioneered, from his office at Rochester's Kodak Park.

Along with endless rolls of film, he developed a joint reputation as a kind, courtly man with a seemly but sumptuous lifestyle, and as a philanthropist whose gifts to education and health care institutions stagger the imagination.

Eastman never married. Other than a housekeeper, eight maids, and a maid for the maids (all well paid, with a then all-but-unheard of two to three weeks vacation each year), the only woman who ever lived in the big house at 900 East Avenue was his elderly mother, who died in 1907. There were also two butlers,

*Film producer Samuel Goldwyn and his wife,
Frances, enjoy a game of cards at their Hollywood
home in the 1930s.*
PHOTO GETTY IMAGES.

as well as whatever auxiliary help was needed on occasions such as New Year's 1914, when nine hundred guests were present at the Eastman mansion.

"A platinum mounted farm," was how one guest described Eastman's estate, for in its early days the mansion and its formal gardens were adjoined by vegetable gardens, greenhouses, and barns for chickens and cows. The "platinum" part of the description refers of course to the house itself, where Eastman rose every morning to the sound of his enormous Aeolian organ, played by his house organist, breakfasted amid potted plants and cut flowers in his airy conservatory, and delighted in showing visitors his billiard room, darkroom, home theater, and trophies from African safaris. And, of course, there was the little upstairs kitchen where Eastman baked his lemon pies.

None of these extravagances precluded Eastman's commitment to philanthropy. He gave away nearly $100 million, including bequests to dental clinics for poor children, Tuskegee Institute, and the University of Rochester. He built his city's Eastman School of Music, and Eastman Theatre. He gave ambulances to France during World War I. And he was the "Mr. Smith"—a mystery for nearly two decades—who financed the core campus buildings of the Massachusetts Institute of Technology. In 1924, he gave $9 million in stock to Kodak employees. "Men who leave their money to be distributed by others are pie-faced mutts," he once remarked. "I want to see the action in my lifetime."

Eastman knew when that lifetime had run its course. At age 77, he was in pain and growing weaker,

the victim of a degenerative spinal disease. He had once asked his doctor to show him exactly where his heart was, and on the afternoon of March 14, 1932, he put a bullet through it. Alongside his bed was a note that read, "To my friends, My work is done— Why wait?"

As all those miles of Eastman motion-picture film spooled through cameras and projectors, they made the fortunes of a group of individuals as tough and determined—and easily as colorful—as any American entrepreneurs before or since. In the 19th century, a showman was a man like P. T. Barnum, who could pack a circus tent or museum of curiosities, or sell out a string of performances by Jenny Lind. Edison and Eastman changed all that, and created a new breed of showman who could reach audiences in hundreds of places at once.

HOLLYWOOD MOGULS

"Poor, poor, poor," was how the man born Shmuel Gelbfisz described his boyhood in the Jewish ghetto of Warsaw. If that description fit the early years of Sam Goldwyn, it could just have easily been applied to Louis B. Mayer, born amid the anti-Jewish pogroms of Czarist Russia, or Jack Warner, born in London, Ontario, after the immigration of his parents from Russia. All of these men came to maturity in the first years of the 20th century, and all of them tried their hands at something else before they got into—or, rather, behind—the movies.

Gelbfisz (he took the name Goldwyn in 1918, after several years as Goldfish) walked 500 miles from

Warsaw to Hamburg, where he took a ship for England before sailing to Canada. Making his way to the United States—again, on foot—he became a successful glove salesman for a firm in Gloversville, New York. One day in Manhattan, he happened to take in a nickelodeon show. He was so fascinated with the new medium of motion pictures that he talked his brother-in-law, Jesse Lasky, into starting a film production business. The founding of Metro-Goldwyn-Mayer (with which he was associated only in 1924, the year it was organized), and a later career as an independent producer all date

to that day when the glove salesman decided to pass an August afternoon watching the "flickers" at the Herald Square Theater on 34th Street.

Louis Mayer (he added the "B." himself, saying it stood for Burt), spent his school days in Saint John, New Brunswick, where his teacher once asked each member of the class what they would do with a thousand dollars. No houses or boats or shopping sprees for Louis—"I'd put it into a business," he answered—or, at least, he later said he did, which may as well be the same thing. The business he soon found

(ABOVE)

Louis B. Mayer, the real roar behind the MGM lion, arrives in the U.S. on the SS Paris, *October 1934.*

PHOTO MGM STUDIOS/COURTESY GETTY IMAGES.

(RIGHT)

Louis B. Mayer's Santa Monica beach house in the 1930s: Mayer's route to this idyll took him from the Ukraine by way of Saint John, New Brunswick, and Haverhill, Massachusetts.

PHOTO GETTY IMAGES.

himself in was scrap metal, his father's trade. On his own in Boston, he followed the same line of work . . . until one day he, too, went to a nickelodeon show. Mayer soon leased a theater in Haverhill, Massachusetts, and started screening the latest films. A chain of picture show venues followed, as did a film distribution business. Then came production, and Mayer's long career with Metro-Goldwyn-Mayer.

Jack Warner and his brothers borrowed against the family horse to buy their first projector, and launched their careers by showing *The Great Train Robbery* on a

bedsheet in Youngstown, Ohio. They opened their first theater in New Castle, Pennsylvania, in 1903. Jack Warner was only 11 years old then, but he would become the driving force of Warner Bros., the production company the brothers founded in 1923. That same year, the Warners signed their first superstar: a war-orphaned German Shepherd named Rin-Tin-Tin. Five years later, they made the movies talk with *The Jazz Singer*.

Collectively, these movie men who had started with nothing came to create a particular image of how

American millionaires were expected to act in the 20th century. It was the southern California version of the plutocrat's lifestyle, a far cry from J. P. Morgan steaming along on the *Corsair* or ensconced in his dark library like a Borgia pope. Jack Warner tooling through Beverly Hills in his Bentley, presiding over cocktails alongside his two swimming pools, or losing a quarter of a million dollars playing Baccarat with King Farouk at Monte Carlo; Louis B. Mayer not only raising but riding prize horses at his ranch, or bragging about slamming through nine holes of golf in an hour, as

(ABOVE)

Jack Warner in 1962, with the two stars of Warner Bros.' Whatever Happened to Baby Jane? *—Bette Davis, left, and Joan Crawford, right.*

PHOTO GETTY IMAGES.

(OPPOSITE)

A film industry luncheon, c. 1925. Louis B. Mayer sits at the head of the table; fifth from left is William Randolph Hearst, seated next to his mistress, actress Marion Davies.

PHOTO GETTY IMAGES.

Walt Disney poses a pair of non-animated subjects—his daughters Sharon and Diane, in the garden of their Los Angeles home.
PHOTO GETTY IMAGES.

if the game was a race—none of this was in the old Newport style. Sam Goldwyn, in his Savile Row suits, might have come the closest to projecting the old upper-class image. It was something he worked hard at: from the time he was a boy, he once said, he had "wanted to be somebody."

WALT DISNEY

Walt Disney's background couldn't have been more different from those of the film pioneers who hailed from the Jewish ghettos of eastern Europe. He was a Protestant Midwestern boy, and like Henry Ford he always placed great stock in the characteristics of that moral and physical terrain of his youth—a world embraced just as fervently by the immigrant movie moguls, as any Andy Hardy film will attest. As Ford did with Greenfield Village, Disney eulogized small-town America in his "Main Street U.S.A." environments at Disneyland in California and Disney World in Florida. But, like Ford, his great contribution to American culture was homogenization. Ford made the shopping mall and the fast-food restaurant possible. Disney filled these places with characters recognizable to everyone. In addition, he made the theme park, rather than raffish old carnivals like the one he depicted in *Dumbo*, the paradigm of American amusement.

Whether or not Walt Disney set out to do these things, or whether they would have emerged anyway as an inevitable consequence of mass tastemaking and mass communications in a democratic society, is almost beside the point of what the man wanted to do with his life and his business. Born in Chicago in 1901, Walter

Rail buff Walt Disney put train rides in his theme parks. At his home he often took guests on his own scale railway.

(ABOVE)
The family behind family entertainment: Walt Disney, c. 1955, with his wife Lillian, daughter Diane, and grandchildren.
PHOTO GETTY IMAGES.

(OPPOSITE)
Howard Hughes with Ginger Rogers.
PHOTO LIBRARY OF CONGRESS.

(PREVIOUS SPREAD)
Rail buff Walt Disney put train rides in his theme parks. At his home he often took guests on his own scale railway.
PHOTO GENE LESTER/GETTY IMAGES.

Elias Disney grew up on a farm in Missouri. In the years just after World War I, he worked as a commercial artist in Kansas City, where he met and briefly went into business with Ub Iwerks, the animation artist who was to be so important to the development of Disney's signature screen products. Disney arrived in Hollywood in 1923, at first hoping to become a film director, but soon landed a contract to create a series of combination live action-animated shorts called *Alice in Cartoonland*. Next came *Oswald the Rabbit*, followed by an idea Disney had for a mouse

named Mortimer. He liked mice; he had once kept several of them as pets in his Kansas City office. Renamed Mickey, and graced with the most famous pair of ears in the history of capitalism, the plucky rodent was launched in a silent short called *Plane Crazy* .

Sound and color, the *Silly Symphonies*, *Snow White*, and all the other full-length features, live action films, nature documentaries, the television programs, and the theme parks—it has become trite to point out that it all began with Mickey Mouse. Just as overworked is the revelation, hardly a surprise to anyone any more, that

Walt Disney didn't, and couldn't, draw Mickey. His genius was not for cartooning, it was for organization.

By the time he reached late middle age, Walt Disney was as rich as, or richer than, many of his moviemaking counterparts, but we must search in vain for any evidence of the flamboyance or conspicuous consumption that often characterized the breed. Disney bought his suits off the rack, not from Savile Row; he was fond of steaks and chili, not the oeuvre of any private French chef, and he bought mid-priced American cars almost until the end of his life. He

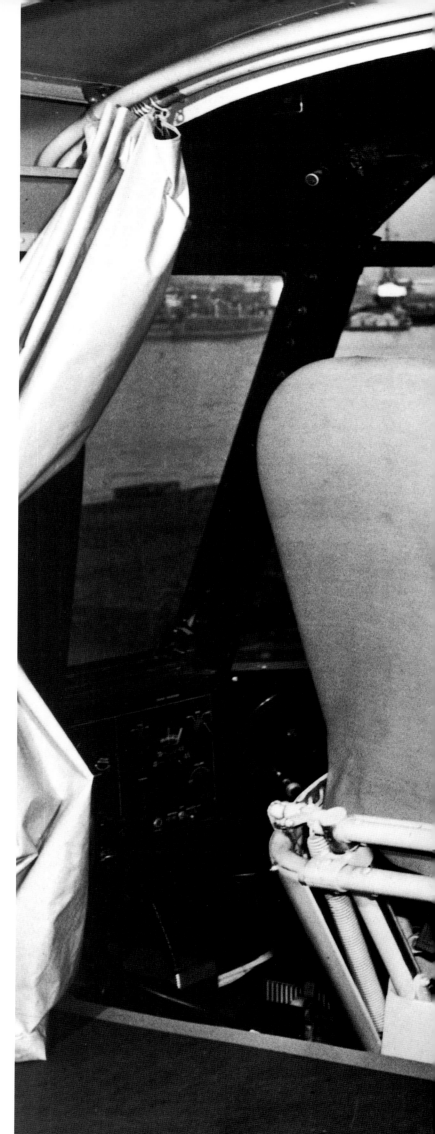

eventually took to driving a Jaguar that had been used in his film *That Darned Cat*, although that departure from custom might be written off as the economy of getting more use out of a paid-for prop. His one expensive indulgence was a half-mile-long model railroad, with rolling stock big enough to ride on, that he constructed on the grounds of his Los Angeles home. Disney puttered endlessly with his train, even after his young daughters grew tired of it; visit the Disney home, and you were likely to get a ride.

Not much fodder there for the modernist sensibility, which would prefer to find, beneath the aggressively wholesome exterior, a rakehell Disney. But all of the man's energies seemed to have been channeled into his work. That work culminated, not surprisingly, in the creation of two model environments — in California and, posthumously, in Florida — as scrupulously engineered as his little home railway.

HOWARD HUGHES

To any American middle-aged or younger, mention of the name Howard Hughes will likely bring to mind the grotesque caricature of a mysterious hermit billionaire, an addled, secrecy-obsessed invalid who spent his days bedridden in darkened rooms, watching the film *Ice Station Zebra* over and over again. This was the portrait of Hughes that emerged during his last days in the early and mid-1970s, when he was at the center of a controversy involving a spurious "as told to" Hughes biography and a shadowy figure in the Byzantine twists of the Watergate affair. Anyone older, though, might recall Hughes as the glamorous titan of the midcentury

film and aircraft industries, a tall, handsome character as closely involved with his leading ladies as he was with test-flying his planes. Such recollections made the image of the scrawny, bearded eccentric with uncut fingernails even more bizarre.

Howard Robard Hughes grew up rich. When he was three, his father invented the rotary bit that would eventually be used to drill three-quarters of the world's oil wells. Young Howard was heir to the Hughes Tool Company, which he used as the springboard to one of America's most spectacular, and most unconventional, business careers. It was also one of the most lucrative: at his peak, Howard Hughes was a billionaire, second in worth only to oilman J. Paul Getty.

Hughes parlayed his father's drill-bit fortune into the creation of the Hughes Aircraft Company, as well as a career as a movie producer and director. He also controlled Trans-World Airlines. Obtaining his pilot's license in 1928, Hughes spent the next two decades enthralling the public with his exploits as a flyer. He set short-distance and transcontinental speed records during the 1930s, and in 1938 circled the world in three days, 19 hours, and 17 minutes, a record that earned him a tickertape parade. A movie fan magazine put him on the cover alongside one of the more serious of his Hollywood romantic interests, posing the question, "Will America's hero, Howard Hughes, marry Katharine Hepburn?" The wedding never took place. And in November 1947, Hughes piloted his wooden-fuselage, eight-engine, 190-ton HK-1, nicknamed the "Spruce Goose," on a 1,000-foot flight that lasted less than a minute. The $40,000 prototype, designed as a troop carrier but never adopted by the U.S. military, has a 320-foot wingspan and was the largest aircraft ever.

What caused Hughes's descent into an eccentricity that finally crossed the line into madness? For one thing, he was the victim of obsessive-compulsive disorder, a form of mental illness that had not yet been described when he began to fuss inordinately over germs, paper tissues, and even the precise half-inch square dimensions he required for the diced vegetables in his beef stew. He also wrestled with drug addiction, which began when he was administered morphine following a near-fatal 1946 plane crash and continued with massive doses of codeine and Valium during his final years. Finally, there was syphilis. Hughes was warned by doctors that he had contracted the primary stage of the disease as early as the 1930s. After his death in 1976, an autopsy showed evidence of tertiary-stage syphilis, which is invariably accompanied by profound mental deterioration.

Howard Hughes slid toward death in fanatically and expensively guarded privacy, over the course of several years in which he holed up in a Las Vegas hotel he owned and, finally, in Acapulco. And yet his protracted demise was paradoxically a public one, followed by a media that picked up on every Gothic tidbit. The fascination was fed by the Watergate angle, having to do with secret Hughes contributions to Richard Nixon's campaigns, and by the bogus biography. But in the end, there was one central story line that held the public rapt: here was a man so rich, and yet so miserable.

Along with Hughes's pioneer aeronautical designs,

one additional engineering contribution was remembered when he died. He had designed a brassiere for Jane Russell to wear in his 1943 film *The Outlaw*.

Although the film tycoons used southern California as the setting for the mammoth extravaganzas of their own life stories, a lesser known but hardly less successful group of men chose a different place in the sun. Henry Flagler, James Deering, and John Ringling couldn't have come about their fortunes through more widely divergent paths. But they all found in

subtropical Florida the ideal setting for extravagant and highly individualistic architectural expression.

HENRY FLAGLER

Although he was instrumental in helping John D. Rockefeller launch the Standard Oil Company, Henry M. Flagler is best known today for what he did with his millions during the latter part of his life. Flagler was the man who first realized the enormous potential of the Florida coast, where he developed destination resorts such as the Royal Poinciana Hotel in Palm Beach and

St. Augustine's Ponce de Leon. He built the Florida East Coast Railway, which eventually leaped across miles of salt water to reach Key West. And when Flagler decided to create his own Florida retreat, he did it in just as grand a style.

Whitehall, Flagler's 55-room, 60,000-square-foot Beaux-Arts extravaganza on Lake Worth in Palm Beach, was completed in 1902 as a gift for the 72-year-old tycoon's third wife, Mary. Built around an open central courtyard, the mansion was designed by Carrère and Hastings—architects of New York's Public Library—and decorated in a variety of Italian Renaissance and French *ancien regime* styles. A red tile roof gives a warm, Mediterranean feeling to the structure that belies its interior formality, which is reinforced by marble floors, damask-covered walls, and a 4,400-square-foot reception hall topped by a painted ceiling depicting "The Crowning of Wisdom."

Visitors to Whitehall, today fully restored as a museum, might nevertheless wonder if the peripatetic Flagler, restlessly at work almost until his death in 1913, might have felt more at home in the smaller quarters preserved adjacent to the great house . . . his private railroad car.

JOHN RINGLING

Ca' d'Zan, in Sarasota, is the house we might expect a great showman to build. John Ringling was one of the five Ringling Brothers, who founded one of the world's most popular circuses in 1884 and eventually bought out their competitor, Barnum and Bailey.

In 1924, at the age of 58, John Ringling started

(RIGHT)

Ca' d'Zan, the Ringling winter residence, 1924–1927. Court (Great Hall).

COLLECTION OF THE JOHN AND MABLE RINGLING MUSEUM OF ART, THE STATE ART MUSEUM OF FLORIDA. PHOTO GIOVANNI LUNARDI, 2002.

(PREVIOUS SPREAD)

Ca' d'Zan the Ringling winter residence, 1924–1927. West façade.

COLLECTION OF THE JOHN AND MABLE RINGLING MUSEUM OF ART, THE STATE ART MUSEUM OF FLORIDA. PHOTO GIOVANNI LUNARDI, 2002.

building his Sarasota winter home. Intending that his showplace also serve to house his Venetian art collection, Ringling and his wife Mable turned to Venice for architectural inspiration, incorporating many of the Gothic elements that characterize the palazzi lining the Grand Canal: one series of columns surrounding a second-floor gallery even suggests a principal motif of the Doges' Palace. The name Ca' d'Zan is likewise Venetian. In the distinctive dialect of the *Serenissima*, it means "house of John"—although today's curators are quick to point out that Mable Ringling had as much to do as her husband with its striking colors and textures. Ca' d'Zan, which cost the Ringlings $1.5 million despite the fact that it is not an immensely large house, is distinctive for its stucco exterior walls in a subtle rose color, its bright marble terraces, and for a wealth of intricate terra cotta detailing on interior as well as exterior surfaces.

Even though he was nearly ruined by the 1929 stock market crash, John Ringling retained a magnificent collection of Baroque paintings, including the world's largest private holding of the work of Peter Paul Rubens. Ca' d'Zan's galleries were opened to the public in 1930, during Ringling's lifetime, and the circus king's quirky, cheerful structure remains a popular museum today.

JAMES DEERING

Fly in low over Biscayne Bay on the approach to Miami International Airport, and one of the most arresting sights below is a particularly ponderous-looking boat moored just offshore from a splendid

(ABOVE)

Ca' d'Zan, the Ringling winter residence,
1924–1927. Ballroom.

COLLECTION OF THE JOHN AND MABLE RINGLING MUSEUM OF ART,
THE STATE ART MUSEUM OF FLORIDA. PHOTO GIOVANNI LUNARDI,
2002.

(OPPOSITE)

Ca' d'Zan, the Ringling winter residence,
1924–1927. West facade tower.

COLLECTION OF THE JOHN AND MABLE RINGLING MUSEUM OF ART,
THE STATE ART MUSEUM OF FLORIDA. PHOTO TERRY SHANK, 2002.

Italian Renaissance villa.

But look again—that boat is filled with marble statuary, and the reason it looks so ponderous is that it, too, is made of stone. The "Great Stone Barge," as it is called, is simply one of many highly individualistic extravagances at Vizcaya, James Deering's bayside estate.

Deering, a vice-president of the International Harvester Company, began building Vizcaya (the Basque name is that of a Spanish province on the Bay of Biscay) in 1916 as the centerpiece of a 180-acre property that included a dairy farm, stables, greenhouses, and 10 acres of formal Italian gardens. Not content with merely replicating the furnishings and architectural elements he admired, Deering and a consultant, artist Paul Chaflin, scoured Europe for the statuary, paneling, mantelpieces, tapestries, and paintings that today make Vizcaya an important museum chronicling some 400 years of art and design.

Vizcaya's Italian Rococo Music Room incorporates walls and ceilings from Milan's Palazzo Borromeo; the tinted plaster ceiling in the Reception Room once adorned the Rossi Palace in Venice. These and other authentic elements are complemented by specially commissioned touches such as an embroidered linen ceiling (in Deering's bathroom); silk wall coverings by Scalamandre; and, in the Tea Room, painted canvas walls depicting classical ruins.

And there is the Great Stone Barge, laden with its allegorical maritime statues by Stirling Calder. It isn't going anywhere, but no matter: James Deering already brought much of the world to Vizcaya.

(RIGHT)

Vizcaya is surrounded by 10 acres of Italian gardens, with typical Renaissance emphasis on symmetrically placed statuary and fountains.

PHOTO COURTESY VIZCAYA ESTATE.

Modern Moguls

UST as Joseph Pulitzer and William Randolph Hearst used advances in printing to create their newspaper and magazine empires, a new breed of media barons built their fortunes on the revolution in wireless communications pioneered by Guglielmo Marconi at the beginning of the 20th century. Although the careers of these czars of mass communications began in the radio days of the 1920s and '30s, they came into the full measure of their power and influence with the postwar arrival of television.

On the night of April 14, 1912, a 21-year-old wireless operator sat at his station in New York's Wanamaker department store. Operated by the Marconi Wireless Telegraph Company, the station was thought of by many people as little more than a gimmick, a clever publicity device for the store. But there was nothing frivolous about the dots and dashes of Morse Code that came across David Sarnoff's earphones that night. They relayed the desperate situation of the White Star liner *Titanic*, foundering in the north Atlantic after a glancing but fatal collision with an iceberg. Sarnoff, manager of the Marconi station, was one of the few people on the east coast of North America with what would later be called a "real time" connection with the disaster.

Impressed as they were with young Sarnoff's coolness and competence as the *Titanic* tragedy played itself out, the young man's superiors were less enthusiastic when he submitted a memorandum, four years later, suggesting that Marconi's wireless technology might outgrow its utilitarian role and make possible a "radio music box," enabling listeners to enjoy "concerts, lectures, music, recitals, etc. which may be going on in the nearest city within their radius." "Harebrained," was one Marconi official's opinion of the idea.

David Sarnoff was too serious a man to harbor harebrained ideas. Born in a Russian Jewish shtetl in 1891, he had sailed in steerage with his family to America, and learned English from newspapers he picked out of the trash on the Lower East Side of Manhattan. He had started

David Sarnoff at the New York World's Fair, 1939. NBC began regular television broadcasts that same year.

with Marconi in 1906, learning Morse Code and wireless operation well enough to advance from office boy to station manager by the time of the *Titanic* sinking. Then, in 1919, he had another opportunity to present his "music box" idea. The Marconi Company had been bought out by a bigger firm, whose initials were to become as much a part of Sarnoff's identity as his own: the Radio Corporation of America.

Sarnoff sold RCA management on the idea of radio broadcasting, and on the business of selling radios. By 1927 he was the man in charge of RCA's fledgling 25-station network, the National Broadcasting Company.

David Sarnoff was not only a radio pioneer, shepherding NBC through the medium's formative years and golden age of popularity in the 1930s and '40s. He was also the visionary and technical wizard who saw the potential of television, and made sure his company had the talent and technology to plunge into the new medium when the time was right. Amazingly, he told his RCA superiors as early as 1923 that television would become "the ultimate and greatest step in mass communications"—a belief that led him, in 1928, to secure a government permit for New York's first experimental television network. Regular programming began in 1939. "Sarnoff was the visionary," CBS executive Frank Stanton later recalled. "He had the guts." In the postwar years, when TV really took off, it was Sarnoff's guts—and gut instincts—that led him to develop an extensive network based on black-and-white broadcasting when rival CBS was still hoping that color would be the entry-level technology.

For all his pioneer involvement with the electronic media that would transform American tastes and lifestyles, David Sarnoff seemed like a tycoon from an earlier era. Formal and formidable, almost stuffy, he easily wore the title "General" earned during his reserve service in World War II, when he built an Allied radio network after the D-Day invasion. He lived in a 30-room Manhattan town house, and ruled his empire from an oak-paneled office with a private barbershop in Rockefeller Center's RCA Building. Perhaps most surprising of all were Sarnoff's cultural tastes. His favorite activity at Rockefeller Center, when he could get away from his desk, was to listen to Arturo Toscanini and the NBC Symphony rehearse. He hated NBC's own "Amos 'n' Andy" radio show, not because it was racist but because it was frivolous. "If comedy is the center of NBC's activities, then maybe I had better quit," he once said. But Sarnoff didn't quit, and more than a few comedies went out across the radio and TV airwaves in his time. He was too good a businessman to have decreed otherwise.

WILLIAM S. PALEY

In the 1950s and '60s, many of the most momentous decisions in the television world—from the airing of landmark documentaries to the development of the frothiest situation comedies—were made around an antique chemin-de-fer gaming table that belonged to a one-time cigar manufacturer named William S. Paley.

Unlike David Sarnoff, who came into radio and television by way of his technical capabilities, Bill Paley got involved in mass communications because of . . .

well, because of cigars. His father manufactured the La Palina brand, and Paley—born in Chicago in 1901— began in 1928 to supervise a show called "The La Palina Smoker" that the family firm sponsored on the shaky young Columbia radio network. Paley had heard the new medium for the first time in 1925, and it fascinated him. Using his share of the proceeds from the family's sale of stock in its cigar company, Paley bought a controlling interest in Columbia in 1928. At 27, he was president of a radio network.

Bill Paley didn't build CBS while grumbling about comedy offerings taking the place of high culture—"I am not a highbrow," he once asserted. "I do not look down on popular taste." Right from the beginning, he went after broad popular appeal, and he went after advertising. Soon after heading for New York to take charge at Columbia headquarters, he signed Paul Whiteman, the era's most successful mass-appeal jazz bandleader. "True Story" soon went on the air as a CBS radio version of the popular pulp magazine. Paley's network brought America George Burns and Gracie Allen, Jack Benny (who would defect to NBC, and then later rejoin the CBS fold) and Fred Allen, and introduced stage superstar Will Rogers to radio. Later, in the mid-1930s, Paley lured Al Jolson, amateur hour host Major Bowes, and Nelson Eddy from NBC.

Babe Paley strikes a characteristically stylish pose as her husband, CBS chief William Paley, frames a photo at the Paleys' Jamaica retreat.
PHOTO GETTY IMAGES.

Meanwhile, he relentlessly courted advertisers such as Chrysler Corporation and American Tobacco.

Paley's talent-scouting expeditions to Manhattan theaters and nightclubs came naturally to a man who was a lifelong bon vivant and big spender. In 1928, flush with his cigar money, he had paid $16,000 for a Hispano-Suiza, one of the most elegant automobiles of that or any age. In 1930, he moved into his first big New York apartment, a triplex that he had redecorated at a cost of $10,000 per room. His bachelor pad had eight radios, a dressing room with a built-in massage table and room for three hundred suits, and a silver-painted barroom with a circular aluminum staircase leading to a roof garden. It was all an Art Deco test run for the house he built after marrying his first wife, Dorothy Hart Hearst (Paley had swept her away from her first husband, Jack Hearst, son of the master of San Simeon). That six-story extravaganza had a black maple floor inlaid with brass, and a staircase carpeted in zebra skins. But the Paleys moved out after only three years. Bill's tastes were growing more refined. He had also begun to collect art. Beginning with Matisse, he eventually acquired works by Lautrec, Cezanne, Gaugin, and Picasso.

Paley would eventually own estates on the north shore of Long Island, at Squam Lake in New Hampshire, and on Lyford Cay in the Bahamas, as well as a spectacular Fifth Avenue apartment. With Dorothy—and, later, with his second wife, best-dressed-list perennial Barbara Cushing "Babe" Paley—he would entertain on a lavish scale. The Long Island place in particular was the scene of weekend parties that prompted one visitor to claim he was "overcome by the brilliance and charm and beauty and style of life at the Paleys'."

But Bill Paley's truest domain was the office from which he ran the Columbia Broadcasting System. After 1964, that antique chemin-de-fer table stood in his private quarters at Black Rock, the sleek, severe CBS headquarters building. By then, Paley's legend was well ensconced in the public imagination: there was the Paley who had built a superb news organization around Edward R. Murrow and his colleagues, the Paley who had earned CBS television its reputation as the "Tiffany Network." It hardly mattered that Paley had not at all been unaided in his accomplishments, that he had held onto his faith in radio long after TV seemed the wave of the future, and that the "Tiffany Network" broadcast series such as "The Beverly Hillbillies" and "Petticoat Junction." The effervescence and drive of the cigar man turned radio whiz was what mattered, so much so that Paley survived, albeit in a diminished role, as a part of CBS management until his death in 1990. A fellow entertainment magnate sized up the old man as well as anyone, remarking after a first meeting that "I have seen pure willpower."

TED TURNER

One summer day in the early 1980s, a traveler dining at a restaurant in the tiny native community of Eskimo Point in Canada's Northwest Territories (now Arviat, Nunavut Territory) looked up from his lunch of caribou stew and whale meat at the television mounted above the bar. The news was on, and an incongruous stream

"Captain Outrageous" Ted Turner—no stranger to rough waters or bold tacking maneuvers— sailing off the Florida coast.
PHOTO KEVIN FLEMING/CORBIS.

of images from the world's capitals and trouble spots pressed its way in upon this subarctic outpost on the shores of Hudson Bay. That was marvel enough, made possible by the big satellite dish planted on the edge of the tundra. But just as remarkable was the phrase in the newscaster's signoff: "from Atlanta." Not Toronto, not Winnipeg, but Atlanta. Why was Atlanta sending the news to Eskimo Point?

The answer was simple: because Ted Turner wanted to send it there, and just about everywhere else. The man called "Captain Outrageous" had been struck by the idea that people shouldn't have to wait until the news came on, but that it should always be on. His answer was the Cable News Network.

The path Turner took to CNN—and to the sale of his media and sports empire to Time-Warner, later AOL Time-Warner—began with his father's outdoor advertising company, which the younger man parlayed into a string of radio stations and, eventually, his entry into the Atlanta television market. When cable and later satellite broadcasting came on the scene, Turner took his Atlanta operation national, creating the first "superstations."

When his countrymen first took notice of Ted Turner, it wasn't because of CNN but because of his fame as a yachtsman. A sailor since boyhood, he took his first national championship in 1963. Captaining *Courageous*, he won the America's Cup in 1977. Around the same time, he was busy establishing credentials in what were, for him, non-participatory sports. He had bought the Atlanta Braves baseball team in 1976, and begun the arduous task of building that organization

Ted Turner's legacy may ultimately rest as much on his vast Western landholdings as on his broadcasting triumphs.

PHOTO JOHN C. AMOS/CORBIS.

into the perennial National League contenders they would become a decade later. In 1977, he bought pro basketball's Atlanta Hawks. With his sports teams and the meteoric growth of Turner Broadcasting, Turner was rapidly becoming the face of the new Atlanta.

He was also, in those days, becoming the "Mouth of the South," known for his freewheeling bluster, shoot-from-the-hip remarks, and good-old-boy insouciance. Having picked up the habit of chewing tobacco from his Braves players, he would work away on a wad, spitting into a glass, while meeting buttoned-down executives from the New York offices of CBS—which, at one point in the early '80s, he attempted to buy. His cigar origins notwithstanding, it isn't easy to imagine Bill Paley chewing tobacco.

Ironically, Ted Turner toned down his flamboyant style during the same decade in which he made headlines through his high-profile marriage (his third) to actress-activist-fitness entrepreneur Jane Fonda. At one World Series after another the two sat in front row seats, doing the Braves' signature "tomahawk chop" (not Fonda's most politically correct moment); and they seemed, as the years passed, like a celebrity institution. But the Turner-Fonda union ended, after 10 years, in 2000. Jane announced that she had become a Christian; Ted had never professed anything stronger than agnosticism. If any of her beliefs had rubbed off on him, they likely had more to do with his growing social activism than with religious dogma.

Ted Turner's ultimate legacy may rest not with his revolutionizing of the television news business, nor with his personal exploits as what the society columns used

to call a "millionaire sportsman." Over the past two decades, what had been a muddled Turner political philosophy has jelled into a commitment to environmentalism and world peace. He gives $50 million each year to his Turner Foundation, and in 1997 announced that he was donating one billion dollars—at the time, roughly a third of his resources—to the United Nations. Parceled out at the rate of $100 million annually for 10 years, the money is to be earmarked for addressing population and women's rights issues, children's welfare, the environment, and global security.

Turner's best gift to America may turn out to be a good part of itself: over the years, he has acquired nearly two million acres of real estate, most of it in the West, making him the nation's largest private landowner. Turner has bought one enormous ranch after another, and has worked hard to restore these properties to pristine condition—removing fences, replanting native vegetation, restocking indigenous animals such as bison. What will be the eventual disposition of landholdings equal in size to Rhode Island and Delaware put together? Turner, in his early sixties, has yet to make public a plan. But given his record of charity and environmental concern, it's difficult to imagine all that land being sold to pay estate taxes, or turned back over to agribusiness and development. It will be interesting to see just what Ted Turner has in mind.

MALCOLM FORBES

It was the evening of May 20, 1986, and a bagpiper was welcoming guests to a Hudson River pier in Manhattan.

Malcolm Forbes cradles one of his collection of Fabergé eggs, crafted for the Russian imperial court.

Alongside the pier lay the magnificent *Highlander V*, a yacht that looked more like a small ocean liner than a large pleasure boat. Like the vessel's name, the bagpiper was a nod to the Scottish antecedents of the man who was celebrating the maiden cruise of his fine new toy. Malcolm Forbes was having a party.

This latest in a line of Forbes yachts named *Highlander* was a toy decked out with toys. Secured to its decks were two speedboats, a Cigarette and a Donzi, alongside launching davits; a Bell Jet Ranger helicopter; and a pair of Forbes's favorite Harley-Davidson motorcycles—he owned more than 60 motorcycles. Inside were sumptuous salons and staterooms, and a restaurant-worthy galley capable of turning out, as it did during that star-studded launch party, a feast of lobster, prime tenderloin, and choice wines. Near the entrance to the main salon stood the man himself, shaking hands and offering cigars. Malcolm Forbes was doing what he did best, having fun.

Highlander was not only the Forbes yacht but the *Forbes* yacht, flagship of an institution which, in the hands of a less flamboyant man, might have been associated more with bottom lines than mooring lines. *Forbes* was—and is—a business magazine, the sort of publication that had traditionally been concerned with making and keeping money rather than with spending it with cheerful abandon. "Capitalist tool," was the puckish sobriquet he gave his publication, standing Marxist cant on its head. But *Forbes* was also its owner's tool for pure enjoyment, his device for turning advertising and circulation into yachts,

hot-air balloons, a castle in Morocco, and even a collection of Fabergé eggs.

Forbes was founded in 1917 by Malcolm Forbes's father, Bertie Charles Forbes, a Scottish immigrant. Malcolm, 35 when his father died in 1954, took over what was a staid and respected publication. Distancing his magazine from the first of those attributes without sacrificing the second, the new publisher ventured increasingly into profiling the

(ABOVE)

In addition to this inflatable, Forbes owned some 60 real Harleys.

(LEFT)

Malcolm Forbes loved balloons, and he loved his stately homes: this temptation was obviously too great.

personalities of American business leaders. He also
introduced the annual *"Forbes* 400" feature, ranking
America's richest individuals in much the same way
that *Fortune* magazine listed leading corporations.

But Malcolm Forbes was destined to be
remembered more for the way he spent his money
than the way he made it. Aside from that succession
of *Highlanders* and his Fabergé eggs, he owned a Fiji
Island, Lauthala; a 40-acre New Jersey estate; a
home along England's River Thames; and a castle in
Tangiers, Morocco. The Tangiers palace was the
location of one of the most talked-about parties of the
1980s, Forbes's 70th—and last—birthday party, in
1989. The publisher flew 1,000 guests to the
celebration, at a cost of $2 million. He appeared in
formal Scottish attire, kilt and all, amid a crowd of
wellwishers that included celebrities as diverse as
Donald Trump, Julio Iglesias, Walter Cronkite, and
Trump's sometime motorcycling companion,
Elizabeth Taylor.

Balloons—not the party kind—were Malcolm
Forbes's abiding passion. He went aloft in a balloon
for the first time in 1972, but by the end of the
following year he had not only qualified as a pilot but
set six world records in hot-air ballooning. In 1974,
he became the first man to fly one of the craft coast-
to-coast across the United States.

The surface of a hot-air balloon, of course,
offers a lot of advertising space. On the record-
setter, the words *"Forbes* " and "Capitalist Tool"
filled it out nicely.

SAM WALTON

If the 1980s had anything to offer in the way of a populist tycoon to counterbalance the image of Malcolm Forbes in his final opulent decade, that individual was a pickup-driving Arkansan named Sam Walton.

By the time Walton died in 1992, he had lead the *Forbes* list as the richest American for seven years. He got there by practicing, and preaching to his employees, the gospel of volume. Walton bought as cheap as he could, sold as cheap as he could, and counted on a vast multiplication of those narrow margins in all of his Wal-Mart stores.

The story of Wal-Mart's origins would have been a familiar one to Frank Woolworth or Rowland Macy, although Sam Walton started on a slightly stouter shoestring than they did. Having worked as a management trainee at a J. C. Penney store before World War II, Walton bought his first store, a Ben Franklin five-and-ten franchise, in Newport, Arkansas. It was 1945, and he was 27 years old.

Having lost his lease on the Newport property, Walton bought a second Ben Franklin franchise in Bentonville, Arkansas, in 1950. Then, two years later, he did what he would keep on doing for the rest of his life: he opened another store. By the early 1960s he had 16 of them, and he had no desire to stop there or anywhere else within sight. And alongside of his commitment to steady growth and high-volume, low-margin retailing, Walton stuck to another principal that many of his colleagues had overlooked. He always located in or near small towns, figuring that such places

had been bypassed by other chains and individual operators but nevertheless offered tremendous opportunities.

In 1962, Walton opened the first store bearing the Wal-Mart name. By the end of the decade, there were 18 of them, along with 14 variety stores Walton still ran under different names (some were still Ben Franklins). All the stores were in the South—in fact, even as late as 1976, all 125 Wal-Marts were within a day's drive of company headquarters in Bentonville.

Wal-Mart, which had gone public in 1970, reached the $1 billion sales plateau 10 years later. The 1980s would be the decade in which Americans outside the South would begin to become aware of Wal-Mart, as the company's expansion reached a pace that put more and more stores well beyond a day's drive of Bentonville (by the century's close, there would be more than three thousand Wal-Mart stores, employing some 825,000 workers).

And it was during the 1980s that Sam Walton became something of a folk legend. The image was one he had shrewdly cultivated within his empire, with his flying visits (often literally, in his small plane) to store after store for pep talks with employees who would be awed by their contact with down-home "Mr. Sam." But Sam Walton really *was* down-home. He bought his shoes—where else?—at Wal-Mart. He never bothered to have his phone number unlisted. His idea of recreation wasn't a trip to the tables at Monte Carlo or racing a 12-meter yacht, but a quail hunt on property he leased in south Texas, where his camp was made up of old trailers. In his aging pickup truck, the rangy, silver-

The Oracle of Omaha: master investor Warren Buffett announces the Disney-Capital Cities merger, 1995.

PHOTO PORTER GIFFORD/LIAISON.

haired Walton looked like a man who had taken a break from his Saturday morning chores to pick up a few necessities in town.

But that's not putting it quite right. In the world he had created, he wouldn't be heading to town, but to the Wal-Mart out on the highway.

WARREN BUFFETT

For one man who has consistently occupied the highest echelons of the *Forbes* list of richest Americans—he often holds second place, behind Bill Gates—the business of making money is not something that follows from providing a particular product or service. It is a function of a finely honed investment strategy that involves many businesses, many products, and many services. Warren Buffett is the consummate investor, and his skill has made him a billionaire many times over.

The son of an Omaha broker, Buffett bought his first stock at age 11. By the time he was in high school his investments, and his skillful management of a chain of paper routes, were paying so well he almost didn't bother with college. But studies at Wharton and at Columbia sharpened Buffett's analytical abilities even more acutely, and by the time he was in his twenties he was busy at his lifetime occupation of beating the Dow. His company, Berkshire Hathaway—named for a textile mill he once controlled—has spawned scores of millionaires, acolytes of the Buffett philosophy of buying sound stocks and holding onto them. At Berkshire's famous annual meetings, rapt investors gather to receive the wisdom of the "Oracle of Omaha."

Equally famous is the Buffett lifestyle, or what most billionaires would consider the lack of one. There are no yachts, no stables of Ferraris, no villas on the Riviera: Warren Buffett still lives in a house he bought for $31,500 over 40 years ago, still wears inexpensive off-the-rack suits, and still favors cherry Coke . . . which tastes even better when you're on the board of directors.

(ABOVE)

An aerial view of the East Hampton, NY waterfront residence of Steven Spielberg.

PHOTO RUSSELL TURIAK/GETTY IMAGES.

(OPPOSITE)

An aerial view of Steven Spielberg's Brentwood home.

PHOTO JAMES AYLOTT/LIAISON.

STEVEN SPIELBERG

Viewers tuning into ABC on the evening of November 13, 1971, might have thought they were in for the usual Saturday night TV movie fare, and at first they saw little to suggest anything different. The week's offering was a made-for-television film called *Duel*, about a motorist pursued across a lonely desert landscape by a homicidal trucker driving an evil-looking 18-wheel gas tanker. More perspicacious viewers, however, might have realized that they weren't merely watching a

standard-grade chase movie slapped together to fill a time slot, but an unusually adept bit of directing — the beginning, perhaps, of a promising career.

The director of *Duel* was a 24-year-old named Steven Spielberg. Ohio-born and raised in New Jersey, Arizona, and California, Spielberg had been fascinated by his father's 8 mm wind-up movie camera, and by '50s TV fare such as "The Twilight Zone and "Davy Crockett." It is doubtful that he ever wanted to be anything but a film director.   He signed his first contract with Universal at 22, having spent much of the preceding year hanging around the studio, using an informally expropriated office and soaking up whatever knowledge and advice he

could by watching other directors at work. That contract led to *Duel*, and *Duel* led to the world beyond television.

A list of the Spielberg films of the subsequent 30 years reads like a history of American popular entertainment in the late 20th century—*Jaws, Close Encounters of the Third Kind, E.T.*, the *Indiana Jones* and *Jurassic Park* series, *Schindler's List*, and *Saving Private Ryan*. Along the way, Spielberg became wealthy beyond the most exaggerated standards of the old Hollywood. By the time the waters had calmed after *Jaws*, his net worth was reported at $200 million, and by the early 1990s he was earning some $70 million per year. "Spielberg is a tycoon, like Rockefeller," Federico Fellini once remarked — but there has never

been any locus with which to associate Spielberg's great wealth, no Kykuit or San Simeon or even anything like the faux-baronial surroundings of earlier Hollywood moguls. Steven Spielberg's personal world, like that of so many of his earlier films, seems rooted in suburban America; his baseball caps and denim jackets come across as less of a pose than something simply comfortable to work in.

GEORGE LUCAS

George Lucas is Steven Spielberg's only serious rival as the master modern mythmaker of American film. Lucas was born in Modesto,

California, in 1944, and as anyone who has seen his *American Graffiti* might suspect, Lucas had a midcentury California kid's passion for drag racing. But not long after high school, he was nearly killed in an auto accident. His dream of racing faded during his months of recuperation—a time during which, legend has it, he began thinking about something called "the Force."

Lucas was part of a new generation who entered the motion picture industry by way of film school. At the University of Southern California, he directed a short called *THX-1138:4EB*, which won a national award and was expanded into a feature in 1970. But it was *American Graffiti*, a paean to hot rods and rock 'n' roll, that launched Lucas's career. The film's success gave him time to work on an idea he had, for a space movie in the old Flash Gordon spirit. After his script was rejected by several studios, Twentieth-Century Fox gave *Star Wars* the go-ahead . . . provided Lucas would trade the usual director's fee for a 40 percent share of the profits, and all merchandising rights.

Any director or producer would be more than satisfied to have devised a franchise as phenomenally successful as *Star Wars*. But one day on a beach in Hawaii, Lucas asked Spielberg if he had ever heard of the Ark of the Covenant. What followed was the *Indiana Jones* Series, like *Star Wars* still a work in progress.

The master of Lucasfilm, and of the special-effects company Industrial Light and Magic, is for all his reported net worth of $3 billion no more of a high-profile spender than his frequent collaborator Steven Spielberg. But Lucas does own a sizeable corner of the world on which he has put his unmistakable stamp. He manages all his wizardry from a 3,000-acre northern California property called, most appropriately, Skywalker Ranch.

HIGH-TECH GIANTS

Henry Ford and John D. Rockefeller were the supreme exponents of the products that defined 20th-century America—the automobile, and the fuel it ran on. Bill Gates and Steve Jobs, two tycoons who rose to phenomenal wealth and power during the century's closing decades, just as succinctly represent our era and its iconic machine.

To carry the analogy further, Gates takes on the role of a latter-day Rockefeller because he makes the software on which most of the world's computers run. And, like Rockefeller, his crucial position as master of one of the most vital components of the world's economy has made him unimaginably wealthy: at the peak stock value of his Microsoft Corporation, William H. Gates III flirted with a net worth of nearly $100 billion, roughly the amount of the U.S. federal budget at the time John Kennedy became president.

Steve Jobs doesn't have that much money (although he is safely a billionaire), nor does he control nearly as large a market share in his part of the industry as Gates does in his. Apple Computer, which Jobs co-founded with Steve Wozniak in 1976, enjoys only a single-digit portion of the personal computer pie. Michael Dell's eponymous machines, which run on Gates's software, are far more common on America's desktops. (Apple

always ran on its own operating system, which it never chose to license—the source, most analysts say, of its stunted growth.)

But Jobs looms large not because he represents some odd Stanley Steamer in a world of Fords. He is part of contemporary business folklore because his first Apple machines did as much as anyone's to create the personal computer market, while his Macintosh and iMac products both reinvigorated it; because he came back from a humiliating forced departure to revive the company he created; and because he has used his visionary genius to transform the animated motion-picture industry through his studio Pixar, producers of *Toy Story* and *A Bug's Life.*

Gates and Jobs display marked differences in style, and in their public projection of themselves. Gates, as the years go by, comes across more and more as the suit-and-tie captain of industry, his image magnified Big Brother style on giant screens above the podiums at which he speaks. Jobs, meanwhile, still cultivates his persona as the intense, offbeat character in jeans and black turtleneck, the Zen-inspired vegetarian who mesmerizes devotees at MacWorld expositions as if he were about to pull a rabbit out of a hat—a feat that, repeatedly throughout his career, he has figuratively accomplished.

But the two men, both born in 1955, have a great deal in common. They started young, and succeeded young. They both inspire fierce loyalty, and intense dislike. Neither suffers fools cheerfully, and each of them determinedly sets the bar for non-foolhood exceptionally high.

LARRY ELLISON

"You can't win without being completely different. When everyone else says we are crazy. I say 'Gee, we must really be onto something.'" The man who made that remark might be different, but few would call him crazy. Larry Ellison launched Oracle Corporation in

Oracle's Larry Ellison is a throwback to the impeccably dressed tycoons of yesteryear.
PHOTO MARTIN KLIMEK.

1977, aiming to revolutionize computer databasing. Oracle grew to dominate the database software market, helping companies like Boeing, Yahoo, Coors, and BMW smoothly manage oceans of vital information. Along the way, CEO Ellison—a college dropout—has become one of the world's richest men. For a while his wealth even surpassed that of his archrival, Bill Gates.

Always impeccable in his $7,000 suits by Armani and Zegna, Ellison cuts a distinctive figure in an industry where it is always "casual Friday." He also fits the mold of the billionaire sportsman soaring over the Pacific in his own Italian fighter jet or racing his 78-foot yacht *Sayonara*. An Asian theme extends to several other passions: he collects Samurai helmets and Chinese ceramics, and lives in a $40-million replica of a Japanese palace complex among the redwoods in California's Silicon Valley nirvana.

JIM CLARK

"All I've ever done," Jim Clark explains, "is build businesses." Clark is the founder of such profoundly influential companies as Silicon Graphics—a pioneer in the field of three-dimensional computer modeling—and Netscape, which helped to transform the World Wide Web from an obscure academic tool to a part of daily life in homes and offices around the world. The personal rewards for these earth-shaking achievements have included a fortune in excess of $500 million, and the most advanced private sailboat ever created—the sailboat *Hyperion*.

To the naked eye, the 155-foot-long vessel is both grandiose and classically elegant, but, by Clark's own admission, "There is nothing that is terribly unique about this boat." The round-bottomed hull shape with its bulb fin keel, and the giant sail that furls into the boom, can be seen on other boats. The mahogany-trimmed staterooms are certainly luxurious, but they hardly represent a revolution in interior design. The ship's captain, Allan Prior, concurs: "There's nothing that's really different from other boats that are built. It's just bigger." Such comments, though, downplay the real wonder of this boat, which begs to be loved not only for its body but for its mind. Behind the scenes of this marvel runs more than 40 miles of copper wire, a central nervous system that collects information on every aspect of *Hyperion*'s operations, and routes it to touch-screen control centers located at 22 separate locations around the ship. A network of Silicon Graphics computers monitors the vessel's engines and generators, its navigation systems, and even its climate controls and video library. It can alert the crew to potential danger, such as changes in hull stresses and weather conditions.

Media coverage of *Hyperion*—which Clark has called "sensational"—has claimed that he will be able to sail the boat by remote control from his desk, halfway around the world. While acknowledging that it's possible, and the boat is prepared for it, Clark and his engineers maintain that this has never been their intention, and they have not even written the necessary software. "You have to ask yourself . . . what is sailing all about?" says systems manager Jim Bokxem. "It would mean that suddenly there is no crew, you step on the boat, push the button, and the boat starts to sail." Where, for a person who loves sailing, would be the fun in that?

BILL GATES

When all is said and done, though, it is the more conventional-seeming Gates who holds the popular imagination, who has become a household word. The reason is simple: he is the richest man in the world.

Bill Gates, a lawyer's son from Seattle, learned the FORTRAN and BASIC computer languages in high school. While he was a student at Harvard in the 1970s, he teamed with his friend Paul Allen to create a form of BASIC for a primitive personal computer called the Altair. Entering into an agreement with Altair's manufacturer to provide the software, the pair in 1975 formed a company they called Microsoft.

Settled into the Seattle suburbs, Microsoft grew throughout the late 1970s as a company that supplied variations of BASIC, FORTRAN, and COBOL for the microprocessors that powered minicomputers—the term then used for machines smaller than mainframes, but still larger than desktop personal computers. In 1981, IBM introduced an initial entry into that field, the PC. At its heart was an operating system supplied by Microsoft, called MS/DOS.

The IBM PC became the paradigm for the personal computer industry as it exploded in size throughout the 1980s and '90s, and MS/DOS followed as the operating system for all of the IBM "clones" that soon came to

Netscape's Jim Clark has built two billion-dollar companies and a sailing yacht as technologically advanced as either of them.
PHOTO © NEIL RABINOWITZ.

dominate home and office computing throughout the world. The success of Microsoft—and of Bill Gates—followed in lockstep with the PC revolution. By 1987, the 32-year-old Microsoft CEO had become the youngest self-made billionaire in history. The ubiquitous Windows platform has since cemented both Microsoft's dominance of the industry, and Gates's place at the top of the Forbes 400 heap (for a short period around the turn of the century, he was displaced by Larry Ellison of Oracle). "Ubiquitous" is in fact an innocuous synonym for the definition of Microsoft which the U.S. Justice Department had on its mind when—shades of Rockefeller's Standard Oil, 1911—it instituted the antitrust proceedings which, as of this writing, are still grinding through the courts.

The media custodians of captain-of-industry folklore like to keep things simple, and "computer nerd" has certainly been a convenient pigeonhole in which to place Bill Gates. The slight frame, the big glasses, the floppy, '70s-style haircut—all of these superficial aspects tend to keep Gates in line with the stereotype.

Tales of Gates's cheeseburger-and-milkshake eating habits have also contributed, as have reports that he drives a Lexus—a coveted car among the upper middle classes, but hardly the chariot of a plutocrat. But there is more here than meets the eye: yes, Gates has included Lexuses among his stable of cars—but they have shared garage space with Ferraris and Porsches, including a Porsche 959 costing nearly $400,000. At this point, of course, price tags are virtually meaningless to Gates.

If, in its superficial way, a Porsche 959 helps mitigate Bill Gates's old computer-nerd image, his charities of recent years have done a great deal to alter the common impression that Gates has been particularly inattentive to the needs of the society that made him so rich. He once remarked that he was saving the task of philanthropy for a later period in his life, but that has changed. Perhaps in response to the chiding of fellow billionaire Ted Turner, whose remark "What good is wealth sitting in the bank?" was aimed in Gates's direction, the Microsoft chairman now doles out vast sums through his Bill and Melissa Gates Foundation. In 2000, the Gates bequests totaled $5 billion dollars.

Where would the richest man in the world live? As for the rest of us, the requirements might be simply stated: a nice private setting, not too far from work. For Gates, this means a four-and-a-half-acre site on Lake Washington, in the Seattle suburbs. He bought the land in the late 1980s and opened the design for his new house to competition. The winning entry was a subtle, contemporary Pacific Northwest–style residence made up of connected pavilions, linked by underground passageways and served by a 20-car garage, a reception hall capable of accommodating more than 100 guests, and a caretaker's house that would easily please a garden-variety millionaire. The home's most striking component, though, is its computerized bank of images—artworks and scenery—that can materialize on wall-sized screens, allowing residents and guests to alter their surroundings at will.

For now, at least, that house on the shores of Lake Washington marks the end of the line in a journey that began on the wharves of Salem, back when the Yankee ships were everywhere.

The Gates' home commands spectacular views of Seattle's Lake Washington. Its exterior features natural materials in traditional Pacific Northwest style, but the technological wonders concealed within include a 22-foot-wide video display composed of 24 rear-projection television monitors, each with a 40-inch screen.

PHOTO MIKE SIEGEL/*SEATTLE TIMES.*

Index